COLLECTING CLUES:
MARGARET ATWOOD'S *BODILY HARM*

Canadian Fiction Studies

Additional volumes are in preparation

Collecting Clues:
MARGARET ATWOOD'S

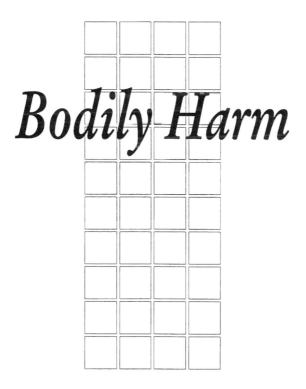

Bodily Harm

Lorna Irvine

ECW PRESS

CANADIAN CATALOGUING IN PUBLICATION DATA

Irvine, Lorna
Collecting clues: Margaret Atwood's Bodily Harm
(Canadian fiction studies ; no. 28)
Includes bibliographic references.
Includes index.
ISBN 1–55022–150–7

1. Atwood, Margaret, 1939– . Bodily Harm.
I. Title. II. Series.

PS8523.A86J437 1993 C813'.54 C90-094509-5
PR9199.3.L38J437 1993

This book has been published with the assistance of the
Ministry of Culture, Recreation and Tourism of the Province
of Ontario, through funds provided by the Ontario
Publishing Centre, and with the assistance of grants from
The Canada Council, the Ontario Arts Council, and the
Government of Canada through the Department of
Communications, and the Canadian Studies and Special Projects
Directorate of the Department of the Secretary of State of Canada.

The cover features a reproduction of the dust-wrapper
from the first edition of Bodily Harm, courtesy of the
Thomas Fisher Rare Book Library, University of Toronto.
Frontispiece photograph by Graeme Gibson.
Design and imaging by ECW Type & Art, Oakville, Ontario.
Printed and bound by Kromar Printing, Winnipeg, Manitoba.

Distributed by General Distribution Services,
30 Lesmill Road, Don Mills, Ontario M3B 2T6.

Published by ECW PRESS,
1980 Queen Street East,
Toronto, Ontario M4L 1J2.

Table of Contents

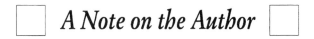

A Note on the Author

Lorna Irvine was born in Ottawa, and attended McMaster and Carleton Universities. In 1977, she received the PhD in Literary Studies from the American University in Washington, D.C., and joined the faculty of George Mason University in Fairfax, Virginia, the following year. She has written articles and reviews on recent Canadian fiction for publications such as *Mosaic*, *Canadian Literature*, *Contemporary Literature*, *Essays on Canadian Writing*, and the *CEA Critic*, and is represented in the collections *Amazing Space: Writing Canadian Women Writing*; *Margaret Atwood: Visions and Forms*; *Probable Fictions: Alice Munro's Narrative Acts*; *The Art of Margaret Atwood*; and *The Lost Tradition: Mothers and Daughters in Literature*. She is the author of *Sub/Version*, published in 1986. She was guest editor of a special edition on women in Canada of *The American Review of Canadian Studies*, is on the editorial board of *Quebec Studies*, and has worked with other scholars to establish various contexts for Canadian literature and criticism within feminist organizations, the Popular Culture Association, the Modern Language Association, and the Association for Canadian Studies in the United States.

NOTE ON REFERENCES AND ACKNOWLEDGEMENTS

The text of *Bodily Harm* used in this study is the original, hardcover edition of the novel, published by McClelland and Stewart in 1981. Page references to this edition are given after quotations.

The author would like to thank the Canadian Embassy in the United States for a Senior Fellowship Award that assisted in the writing of this commentary and George Mason University for additional financial and intellectual support. I am also grateful to the staff of the Thomas Fisher Rare Book Library in Toronto, who helped me become familiar with the Margaret Atwood Archives. Particular thanks go to Judith McCombs and Carole L. Palmer, who allowed me to go through their extensive collection of reviews and articles on *Bodily Harm*, to use their translations of commentary in foreign languages on the novel, and to read McCombs's Literary Introduction, all before the publication of their *Margaret Atwood: A Reference Guide*. I appreciate the careful readings done of early drafts of the manuscript by Laura Tracy and Judith McCombs. And last, I would like to thank Robert Lecker for his continued support of my work.

Collecting Clues: Margaret Atwood's *Bodily Harm*

Chronology

1939   Born November 18 in Ottawa; mother, Margaret Dorothy Killam; father, Carl Edmund; brother, Harold, born in 1937; sister, Ruth, born in 1951.

1940–51   Lived in Ottawa and Sault Ste. Marie; spent summers in Quebec and Ontario bush country; juvenile poem, "Rhyming Cats," published in 1945; family moved to Toronto in 1946.

1952–57   Attended Leaside High School in Toronto.

1957–61   Attended Victoria College, University of Toronto. Teachers were Jay MacPherson, Northrop Frye, Millar MacLure, Kathleen Coburn. Contributed poems and prose to college magazines. Poems published in *Canadian Forum*, *Alphabet*, *Jargon*, *Tamarack Review*. Read poetry at Toronto's Bohemian Embassy, appearing sometimes with Sylvia Tyson.

1961   Published *Double Persephone*, a privately printed chapbook. Won E.J. Pratt Medal for Poetry.

1961–62   Graduated in Honours English from the University of Toronto; awarded Woodrow Wilson Fellowship. Enrolled at Radcliffe where she received an M.A. in English.

1962–63   Began PhD work at Harvard. Met James Polk. Returned to Toronto. Wrote first novel, *Up in the Air So Blue*.

1964   Wrote libretto for *Trumpets of Summer*, a choral suite with music by John Beckwith, commissioned by the CBC.

1964–65   First draft of *The Edible Woman*. Lectured in English at the University of British Columbia. Published *Kaleidoscopes Baroque* and *Talismans for Children*, both illustrated by Charles Pachter.

1965–67	Continued doctoral studies at Harvard.
1966	Published *The Circle Game* (poetry). Awarded the President's Medal for Poetry, University of Western Ontario. Wrote *The Deaths of Animals/The Nature Hut*, unpublished novel.
1967	Received Governor General's Award for *The Circle Game*. Won Centennial Commission Poetry Competition for *The Animals in That Country*. Married James Polk. Taught at George Williams University, Montreal.
1968	Published *The Animals in That Country* (poetry).
1969	Published *The Edible Woman* (novel).
1970	Awarded Union Poetry Prize by *Poetry* (Chicago) for five poems from *Procedures for Underground*. Wrote screenplay for *The Edible Woman* (not produced). Published *The Journals of Susanna Moodie* (poetry) and *Procedures for Underground* (poetry).
1971	Published *Power Politics* (poetry). Joined board of House of Anansi Press. Taught at York University.
1972	Published *Surfacing* (novel) and *Survival: A Thematic Guide to Canadian Literature* (criticism). Writer in Residence, University of Toronto.
1973	Moved to Alliston with writer, Graeme Gibson. Honorary degree from Trent University. Joined Board of Directors of the Canadian Civil Liberties Union.
1974	Published *You Are Happy* (poetry). Won *Poetry*'s Bess Hopkins Prize. Wrote script for CBC television play "The Servant Girl." LLD from Queen's.
1976	Published *Lady Oracle* (novel) and *Selected Poems* (poetry). Daughter Eleanor Jess born.
1977	Published *Dancing Girls* (short stories) and *Days of the Rebels: 1815–1840* (history). Received City of Toronto Book Award and the Canadian Booksellers' Association Award, both for *Lady Oracle*. Won St. Lawrence Medal for *Dancing Girls*.
1978	Published *Two-Headed Poems* (poetry) and *Up in the Tree* (children's story). Visited Australia and Afghanistan.

Lived in Scotland.

1979   Published *Life Before Man* (novel).

1980   Published *Anna's Pet* (children's story). Awarded the Radcliffe Graduate Medal. Moved to Toronto. Honorary Degree from Concordia.

1981   Published *True Stories* (poetry) and *Bodily Harm* (novel). Awarded Molson Prize and Guggenheim Fellowship. Made a Companion of the Order of Canada.

1982   President of the Writer's Union of Canada. Published *Second Words: Selected Critical Prose* and edited *The New Oxford Book of Canadian Verse in English*. Awarded Welsh Arts Council International Prize; honorary degree, Smith College.

1983   Published *Murder in the Dark* (short fictions and prose poems) and *Bluebeard's Egg* (short stories). Honorary Degree, University of Toronto.

1984   Published *Interlunar* (poetry). President of P.E.N. International, Canadian Centre, Anglophone.

1985   Published *The Handmaid's Tale* (novel), which won the Arthur C. Clarke science fiction award and was short-listed for the Booker Prize. Honorary degrees from Mount Holyoke, the University of Waterloo, and the University of Guelph.

1986   Published *Selected Poems II* and co-edited *The Oxford Book of Canadian Short Stories in English*. Won the Toronto Arts Award and the Governor General's Award, both for *The Handmaid's Tale*. Received the Ida Nudel Humanitarian Award of the Canadian Jewish Congress.

1987   Published *The CanLit Foodbook* ("From pen to palate — a collection of tasty literary fare"). Elected Fellow of the Royal Society of Canada; received American Humanist of the Year Award and was named *Ms.* magazine's Woman of the Year.

1988   Published *Cat's Eye* (novel). Inducted as Foreign Honorary Member, Literature, the American Academy of Arts and Sciences.

1989   Short-listed for the Booker Prize for *Cat's Eye*. Received

Canadian Club Arts and Letters Award and the Foundation for the Advancement of Canadian Letters Book-of-the-year Award, both for *Cat's Eye*. Named Author-of-the-year, Canadian Booksellers Association.

1990   Film version of *The Handmaid's Tale*, script by Harold Pinter. Received the Order of Ontario and the Harvard Centennial Medal. Published *Selected Poems: 1966–1984*.

1991   Published *Wilderness Tips* (short stories).

1993   Published *The Robber Bride* (novel).

The Importance of the Work

Bodily Harm's importance resides in its fugal arrangement of profoundly felt political themes and images, and in its attention to ways
of seeing. Although all of Atwood's work concentrates on misuses
of power, this novel effectively links story-telling and nationalism in
an effort to broaden borders. This is the first of Atwood's novels to
investigate fully a "foreign" perspective. The Central America
Atwood creates stands in stark contrast to North America. As the
author said in a 1979 interview: in Latin America "writing a poem
can be an act of enormous courage because the penalty for doing so
could be death" (Ingersoll 119). Bodies in *Bodily Harm*, broken into
pieces, tortured, seem to me to speak more eloquently, and more
obsessively, than those in earlier works, and although they lead to
those in *The Handmaid's Tale*, here, where medicine and politics so
ambiguously mingle, Atwood has brilliantly exposed not what might
happen, but what *is* happening. Joining *Life Before Man*'s concern
with domestic relationships to *The Handmaid's Tale*'s more international themes, *Bodily Harm* reveals politics everywhere, in everything. The characters move between domestic space, with its gender
concerns, and foreign space, where gender also figures loudly and
persistently as power acts out its various scenarios.

Impressed with *Ways of Seeing*, the book that emerged from John
Berger's television series on art, Atwood explores in *Bodily Harm*,
both formally and thematically, fiction's reliance on perspective. Like
Berger, who questions the "relation between what we see and what
we know" (7), she demonstrates how seeing is determined by knowledge and belief, and therefore by national and gender affinities. The
novel's scenario, and its epigraph, reflect Berger's conviction, arrived
at from looking at visual images, that "a man's presence suggests what
he is capable of doing to you or for you. . . . By contrast, a woman's
presence . . . defines what can and cannot be done to her" (45–46);

the "confined space" of woman's existence is demonstrated again and again in the novel's internalized perspective. The divided female self, described by Berger as the "*surveyor* and the *surveyed*" (46), is dramatically portrayed through narrative shifts between first and third person. Even the novel's attention to superficial journalism emphasizes Berger's point that in the contemporary world, media publicity encourages people to believe that sophistication is to "live beyond conflict" (150). *Bodily Harm*'s Dr. Minnow understands that such publicity functions as a tool of capitalism.

When talking to Beatrice Lyons about *Bodily Harm*, Atwood admitted that she had "wanted to take somebody from our society where the forefront preoccupations are your appearance," in order to make clear "that's not the way people in those other countries think, because they can't afford to. They are thinking what is going to happen tomorrow or next week, how they will get through the immediate time. I wanted to take someone from our society and put her into *that*, cause a resonance there" (Ingersoll 227). The disruptions in the text of *Bodily Harm* emphasize the ways in which seeing and speaking differ between Canada and the Caribbean. The narrative voice is necessarily split and what superficially seems to some readers as an unbelievable manipulation of space becomes, rather, a profoundly realized construction of how political commitment evolves. Time too, as it does in "Postcard" (TS), jumps bewilderingly and erratically. Immediate events affect both memory and action, so that plotting seems sometimes deceptive, often artificial. The author repeatedly draws attention to the creating and telling of stories.

This novel, too, pays close attention to breast cancer. The mastectomy that occurs in its pages is not a minor theme. Some critics have found the equation between one woman's fight with cancer and the world's political cancer hackneyed and trivializing. It is neither. By describing the actual opening up of a female body, Atwood has made utterly convincing the "bodily harm" that precedes an understanding of the physical agony that accompanies a politics of repression. The stories of the novel come from a wounded body, from immediate suffering, from current affairs. Atwood's impressive contribution to contemporary fiction is nowhere more completely realized than in this novel, where politics and bodies intimately join, where "seeing" differently through the medium of stories means acting differently. No one is immune. We are all involved.

Critical Reception

To some degree, reviews and critiques of Atwood's *oeuvre* reveal different emphases depending on the situation of the writer. In "Country, Politics and Gender in Canadian Studies," Judith McCombs investigates a wide number of reviews and articles devoted to Atwood's work. Apart from suggesting that many early reviews concentrate on the writer's or the work's degree of "warmth," McCombs argues that reviewers gradually began also to stress nationalist and feminist issues. In her introduction to *Critical Essays on Margaret Atwood*, McCombs points to several differences between Canadian reviews of *Bodily Harm* and those from the United States, the former being usually more serious and informed.

Reviewed by almost all the major newspapers and news journals in the United States, *Bodily Harm* initiated responses ranging from accusations about the novel's banality and bleakness, to praise for its political acumen, its acerbic wit, and its superb orchestration of images and themes. Some of these reviews reveal attitudes to Canada that clearly influenced the reading of the novel. For example, Susan Ager, in the *San Jose Mercury* refers to Atwood's imagination as as "flashy as Ontario in October, as crisp as a Canadian flag and sometimes as chilling as the winter wind over Lake Superior," while Katherine Guckengerger, in the *Cincinnati Enquirer*, finds that the "jazzy change of setting from Canada to the Caribbean is as unsettling as an Eskimo in a hula skirt." Other reviews vary considerably in their tolerance to what they see as Atwood's didacticism. *Publisher's Weekly* speaks of overkill, while the novel's apparent exaggerations, according to Jonathan Penner of the *Washington Post Book World*, can hardly be taken seriously. Many of these reviews note the parallels between cancer's malignancy and the political issues dramatized in the novel, using words like "dissection," describing the characters as "fragmented parts of a human body" and talking about "decay." The novel's damning judgements on American political involvement in Central America make some reviewers uneasy. Diana Ketcham, of the *Oakland Tribune*, castigates Atwood for "equating individual female misfortunes (cancer, mastectomy, sexual abandonment, childlessness, rape)" with the "ills of history," and accuses her of exploiting "the real political tragedies of the third world by using them as symbols of American angst."

On the other hand, John Leonard, of the influential *New York Times Book Review*, calls *Bodily Harm* "an eloquent, gnarled, ugly sermon," and congratulates Atwood for the way in which she has rejected lyricism to present human atrocity. He writes: "For the hummingbirds of her poetry she has substituted crabs, signifying cancer. The severed hands are semaphoric" (21). Reviews written by some women writers seem particularly perceptive. Jill Robinson reads *Bodily Harm* as a "major war novel," Carolyn See believes that the novel reveals that the "compulsive suffering of women has something to do with the compulsive cruelty of men," and Anne Tyler, although not entirely satisfied with the novel, suggests that it must be read twice to be appreciated. She comments on "the numb flatness of a cancer patient's despair, the unconscious hilarity of a tiny, insular, multinational culture, and the chill of the traveler's 'alien reaction paranoia.'"

The Canadian reviews are marked by a tendency to compare *Bodily Harm* with other more or less political novels, such as Joseph Conrad's *Heart of Darkness*, Graham Greene's *The Quiet American*, Paul Theroux's *The Mosquito Coast*, Joan Didion's *A Book of Common Prayer*, Malcolm Lowry's *Under the Volcano*, and various novels by V.S. Naipaul. Others concentrate on comparing its feminist slant with that in the work of Adrienne Rich, Sylvia Plath, Simone de Beauvoir and Jane Rule. Several reviews comment on the parallels between *Bodily Harm* and Susan Sontag's *Illness as Metaphor*. Such comparisons clearly emphasize Atwood's connection to other established authors, and link Canadian literature with famous work from other countries, giving it an international flavour. Along this line, for example, Frank Davey, in the *Canadian Forum*, insists that *Bodily Harm* demonstrates a narrative pattern similar to that of Shakespearean comedy. Many Canadian reviewers pay equal attention to the author and her work by including interviews. Several critics applaud

Atwood for moving into a world of action different from that usually constructed for women characters while, in *Queen's Quarterly*, George Woodcock stresses *Bodily Harm*'s importance, showing its closeness to certain Atwood poems. The cross-referencing of Atwood's work done by Woodcock is common to these reviews, obviously because reviewers know Atwood's work well. The Canadian reviews almost unanimously praise the novel, although the few exceptions, like many of the American reviews, criticize a perceived didacticism. J.A. Wainwright, in the *Dalhousie Review*, insists that Atwood takes a "sledgehammer approach to relationships between the sexes" (581), and *Saturday Night*'s Urjo Kareda evinces uneasiness about Rennie's unbelievable rebirth.

Although fewer, reviews from countries other than Canada and the United States vary widely. Several reviewers castigate Atwood for using hackneyed literary themes, for example, paralleling contemporary western life with cancer or, à la Graham Greene, using the metaphor of the island as hell. References to Canada punctuate some reviews. John Mellors of *London Magazine* congratulates Atwood on revealing to the British "the stunning boredom and self-righteousness of a small town in Ontario" (61), and observes that Atwood's work shows how Canadians can "escape inwards or outwards. Inwards to the primitive 'life before man' of the remote past or of their own almost deserted forests and lakes, outwards to a sophisticated or exotic 'abroad' " (62). Jaidev, the reviewer for *Newstime* speaks of the novel's "disturbing extension of the implication of the feminine to cover the weak of the world." A Swiss review believes Rennie's struggle to be painfully real, a German one praises Atwood's new world freshness, seeing Rennie as a representative Amazon, and another compliments *Bodily Harm*'s union of male and female themes. Marion Halligan, of *The Canberra Times*, focuses on language, describing Atwood's prose as a "kind of highly-wrought vernacular," while Diana Brydon, reviewing the novel for *Westerly*, tells us that the novel's island setting is used mostly to illustrate North American life and that Rennie is meant to alienate readers so that they will look at themselves more critically.

Together, reviews of *Bodily Harm*, most of them from 1981 and 1982, demonstrate Atwood's growing popular reputation at the beginning of the 1980s, and indicate some national differences in approaching the novel's politics, in placing it within a Canadian literary canon, and in seeing it as part of Atwood's growing *oeuvre*. Differently positioned and extending over a much longer time period, scholarly criticism is more affected by its audience and the nature of the publication in which it appears. Arguments differ according to whether references to *Bodily Harm* constitute only part of a more general literary discussion, are a segment of a single-authored book devoted to Atwood's work, occur in a comparative essay, or take up the whole of an analysis devoted solely to the one novel.

In *A Climate Charged*, an investigation of a number of Canadian writers and therefore of the first category, B.W. Powe charges Atwood with using *Bodily Harm* to display fashionable, rather than profound, concerns. Although he compliments her extended metaphors, particularly the multi-levelled use of cancer, Powe believes that much of the novel rehashes the victim theme popularized in Atwood's notorious *Survival*. He finds the characters hollow; always in the process of self-discovery, they do not arrive anywhere. He argues that the whole novel mocks serious political commitment by espousing the "safe turf of anti-colonialism, anti-dictatorship, anti-violence, and anti-censorship" (149), betraying what might possibly be a "Canadian" failure of the moral imagination. Clearly irritated by Powe's somewhat one-sided attack, Linda Hutcheon responds in *The Canadian Postmodern*, by arguing *Bodily Harm*'s powerful social critique, its meticulous diagramming of physical, psychological, and ideological violation, and its challenge to male definitions of the self. Both critics emphasize the novel's political focus. So does Coral Ann Howells in the Atwood chapter of *Private and Fictional Worlds*, where she calls *Bodily Harm* radical and suggests that its feminism merges with the broader issues of nationalism and colonialism.

Other critics in this category tend to downplay the politics of the novel. *Bodily Harm* amply illustrates Roberta Rubenstein's psycho-analytic thesis in *Boundaries of the Self*, that female characters often display ambiguous borders that reflect and extend such devices as irony, ambiguity, and paradox. W. J. Keith castigates critics for using extraneous material to discuss *Bodily Harm*. In *A Sense of Style*, he insists that this novel lacks artistry both because of its abrupt voice shifts and because Rennie's development from excessive naïveté to subversion seems morally anti-climactic. The novel's plot-line confuses him, and though he grants the novel ambitiousness, he judges it seriously flawed. Many critics and reviewers agree with him, insisting that *Bodily Harm* awkwardly links politics and art.

In the second category, the single-authored studies of Atwood's work, four stand out, and as might be expected of work devoted to one author, tend to be laudatory. Jerome Rosenberg (*Margaret Atwood*) looks at *Bodily Harm* through the lens of Atwood's involvement with Amnesty International, the graphic discussions of torture in *True Stories*, the treatment of rape in "Rape Fantasies," the ominous threat that hangs over "When It Happens," and the impending cannibalism in "A Travel Piece." He calls *Bodily Harm* a work of "political realism" (130), evidence of Atwood's developing commitment, although he admits to being distanced from Rennie and troubled because of the apparent failure of language. In his *Margaret Atwood: A Feminist Poetics*, Frank Davey fits *Bodily Harm* into a recurring Atwood narrative pattern in which the main character moves from disruption, through a healing green world, to a restored society. While insisting that Atwood is not political, being more concerned with individual redemption than with social change, Davey implies that Rennie represents all women in her connection with some pre-linguistic female space. This reading, while slightly comforting, ignores the disruptive political messages at the novel's core. Because of its emphasis on myth, Barbara Rigney's *Margaret Atwood* resembles Davey's study. Stressing rebirth, she argues that Rennie must pass through myth and magic, but, sensitive to feminist politics, Rigney emphasizes that female bonding alters Rennie's vision. Ildikó de Papp Carrington, in *Margaret Atwood and Her Works*, pays attention to the structure of *Bodily Harm*. She quotes Atwood's comment that the novel is an "anti-thriller" — the thriller pulled inside out — and suggests that the "satire of the thriller form is not only imposed on the basic romance structure underneath but derives its satiric punch from that structure" (30). Like other critics and reviewers, Carrington points out *Survival*'s influence and, paying attention to the novel's political themes, insists that the responsibility of the writer self-consciously dominates the tensions of the text.

These four books often emphasize connections rather than striking differences among the author's work. They tend to approach individual works developmentally, and are particularly helpful in showing readers *Bodily Harm*'s position in the Atwood landscape. But on the whole, isolated essays offer more radical readings. Two comparative analyses in the third category stand out. In response to Jennifer Strauss's " 'Everyone is in Politics': Margaret Atwood's *Bodily Harm* and Blanche d'Alpuget's *Turtle Beach*," in which Strauss argues for an essentially realistic *Bodily Harm* more structurally sophisticated than the Australian d'Alpuget's *Turtle Beach*, Helen Tiffin ("Voice and Form") mounts a persuasive attack on *Bodily Harm*'s formal properties. Tiffin situates the novel within the context of postcolonial fiction, in which characters function ambiguously as both central and peripheral, dominators as well as victims. According to Tiffin, such ambiguity should create a multicultural perspective. *Bodily Harm*, however, betrays a solitary voice that, Tiffin says, presents western interpretation, definition, and judgement as universal.

Bodily Harm invites the kind of argument engaged in by Strauss and Tiffin, and more exchanges of this sort would increase understanding of the novel. Beryl Langer's "Class and Gender in Margaret Atwood's Fiction," while not structured as a dialogue, also pointedly argues with other readings of *Bodily Harm*. Suggesting that critics have not looked seriously at class issues in Atwood's novels, Langer asserts that Atwood deals with a new social class whose members are confronted with social and moral dilemmas. According to Langer, Atwood's work can be read as a critique of capitalism; until right at the end of the novel, Rennie's relationships, dictated by the marketplace, are superficial. To support her argument, Langer investigates the novel's language closely, although she pays little attention to its obsession with bodies and with harm, and does not develop the possibility that stories, as for example Lawrence Thornton implies they do in *Imagining Argentina*, may bring about political change. Ken Goodwin does articulate the two-way metaphor of body and state in "Revolution as Bodily Fiction: Thea Astely and Margaret Atwood." He shows how Atwood's novel points in different directions in space and time, and suggests that Rennie's operation and Ste. Agathe's efforts to secede from St. Antoine parallel each other. Copies of two Atwood water-colors illustrate Goodwin's essay. These are discussed in Sharon Wilson's "A Note on Margaret Atwood's Visual Art and *Bodily Harm*," which follows Goodwin's essay.

Each of these essays engages with the novel on many levels. Geraldine Finn's "Feminism and Fiction: In Praise of Praxis, Beyond *Bodily Harm*," although also focussed on politics, works less well. Finn clearly wants a different kind of novel, one that would concentrate on women's issues as, for example, writers such as Margaret Laurence, Audrey Thomas, and Alice Munro do. She wants Atwood to show her readers how women could live differently and, like Powe, objects to Atwood's concentration on process over product. Similar objections crop up among other radical feminist critics, who want Atwood to invent new forms to distance herself absolutely from male-dominated narrative structures. From a different political perspective, Larry MacDonald, in "Psychologism and the Philosophy of Progress: The Recent Fiction of MacLennan, Davies and Atwood," castigates Atwood, along with the other two authors, for writing "thesis novels which self-consciously anatomize Canadian society in terms of their writers' deliberately advanced ideas about what is wrong with the social order" (121) MacDonald singles out Atwood for her frequent caricatures of left-wing nationalism, and *Bodily Harm* in particular for its apparent sacrifice of immediacy and density in favour of vagueness and muddle. MacDonald dislikes the way that Atwood collapses distinctions between subjects and objects, a tendency that other critics have also attacked.

As to other more favourable comparative readings, Roberta Rubenstein's "Bodily Harm: Paranoid Vision in Contemporary Fiction by Women," offers some provocative connections between narrative structure and psychoanalysis. Rubenstein stresses that Atwood's creation of worlds hostile to women, linked to the common poststructuralist breakdown of distinctions between the real and the fictional, creates paranoia and a free-floating anxiety notable in much women's fiction. Because it dramatizes uncertainties about what is *really* happening and illustrates a violent outer world impinging on a disturbed inner one, only a narrative style such as that used in *Bodily Harm*, with its shifts from first to third person, and its alternating verb tenses, can replicate paranoia and anxiety. Rubenstein also underscores the novel's linkage of female erotic desire and violence. By suggesting the dangers of female sexuality, this connection leads Rubenstein into positing "penis fear" (147) as constitutive in a female development that produces the victim mentality so frequently illustrated in Atwood's work.

Psychoanalytic readings are particularly valuable when critics pay attention to narrative language and structure, as Rubenstein has done. Sharon Wilson, while emphasizing metamorphosis, also connects image and structure. In "Camera Images in Margaret Atwood's Novels," Wilson investigates the relevance of photography to *Bodily Harm*'s time and space, tracing images from those that remain neutral records of a fragmented and frozen vision, to those that exhibit Rennie's break from the static frame into movement. Although Rennie's physical thawing may be difficult to place, Wilson's attention to seeing, like that of Berger who has also written about photography, underlines Atwood's startlingly visual imagination.

Thematic analyses that include *Bodily Harm*, such as Catherine Rainwater's "The Sense of the Flesh in Four Novels by Margaret Atwood," in which ambiguous physical boundaries are singled out for comment, and Nora Foster Stovel's "Reflections on Mirror Images: Double and Identity in the Novels of Margaret Atwood," in which Stovel suggests an affirming movement from mirrors to windows in the writer's development, remain good introductions for students. So, too, is Rowland Smith's "Margaret Atwood and the City: Style and Substance in *Bodily Harm* and *Bluebeard's Egg*." Smith finds that the shifts in perspective experienced by Rennie are new to Atwood's work. In "Narratives of Survival," Linda Howe fleetingly mentions *Bodily Harm* with other women's *bildungsroman* which emphasize survival, although Howe believes Rennie's survival to be based more on luck than on active involvement. Mentioning *Bodily Harm* in "Tropical Traumas: Images of the Caribbean in Recent Canadian Fiction," Stanley Atherton points out the marked contrasts between northern and tropical landscapes, and insists that Rennie, an outsider in the Caribbean's tropical world, must cling to "what is reasonably and 'Canadianly' normal" (14). As a result, he argues, Rennie's rebirth fails to convince us. In these comparative articles, critics tend to single out recurring and general structural, contextual, and stylistic patterns.

Essays of the final category, those devoted solely to *Bodily Harm*, are more likely to investigate the novel closely, and to avoid sweeping generalizations. One of the best early readings is Elaine Tuttle Hansen's "Fiction and (Post) Feminism in Atwood's *Bodily Harm*," a meticulous discussion of the narrative discrepancies and open-endedness that prevent "univocal authority" (6) in the novel. Hansen terms the dialogue between Rennie and Lora "consciousness raising" and suggests that, by the end of the novel, Rennie has replaced the doctors by becoming a healer herself. Like subsequent critiques, this one raises questions about *Bodily Harm*'s ability to effect social, rather than simply individual, change. Roberta Rubenstein, in "Pandora's Box and Female Survival: Margaret Atwood's *Bodily Harm*," traces the novel's themes of "sex, power, violence, and death" (261) as they bring about Rennie's acceptance of responsibility and her recognition of the power of mothers. Rubenstein believes that Rennie learns the meaning of the hope left in the mythical Pandora's box. Arnold Davidson's "The Politics of Pain in Margaret Atwood's *Bodily Harm*" further evokes the novel's depth, although Davidson asserts more strongly than Hansen the author's control of her material. Using the novel's emphasis on pain to suggest Atwood's criticism of escape fiction and her belief in the necessity of confrontation, Davidson shows that Atwood self-consciously refuses her readers a happy ending, choosing instead an indeterminate one that marks a new kind of reporting for both author and character. Unlike some essays on the novel, Davidson's helpfully addresses the work of other Atwood scholars.

Several essays concentrate on the subject of tourism. Marilyn Patton's "Tourists and Terrorists: The Creation of *Bodily Harm*," particularly valuable because it discusses material from the Atwood archives, carefully diagrams the development of two of the novel's crucial scenes, showing an increasing political emphasis in each draft. Like Davidson, Patton interprets *Bodily Harm* as a model for the kind of writing Rennie imagines as "subversive," and goes farther than Davidson in showing the novel's indictment of the United States's massive involvement in foreign policy as a kind of cannibalism. Earlier, and briefer, readings of *Bodily Harm*'s tourist perspective can be found in the 1982 issue of *Canadian Literature* containing Atherton's essay, discussed above. Reviewing the novel, Clark Blaise finds the Caribbean material poorly integrated and although he believes *Bodily Harm* to be Atwood's most serious novel to that date, he complains about the distracting parallels between personal illness and political disease. As her title makes clear ("Caribbean Revolution and Literary Convention"), Diana Brydon concentrates on the novel's language and the literary conventions Atwood uses to contain revolution. She writes that the novel reveals that "the language of contemporary pop culture poses the greatest threat to Canadian writing" (182), and suggests that *Bodily Harm* parodies the "imperialist novel" (184) by contradicting conventional confrontations with a heart of darkness.

Other essays are worth mentioning because they deal with themes and images either ignored or discussed only superficially elsewhere. In "The Thematic Imperative: Didactic Characterization in *Bodily Harm*," Mary Kirtz stresses the metonymic and ambivalent function of hands throughout the novel, while Catherine McLay, in "The Real Story," argues, not very convincingly, *Bodily Harm*'s differences from earlier Atwood novels. I mention McLay's reading only because it talks about the novel's obsession with surfaces, an obsession shared by its readers as they try to discover the "real" story. In an early (1983) essay, "Another Symbolic Descent," Carrington comments on the novel's submarine spaces as they connect with the underground settings of earlier Atwood stories and poems. She connects Lora's resuscitation with the birth in the story "Giving Birth," and locates the beginning of Rennie's "tourist mentality" in her early objectification of her mother and grandmother. Dorothy Jones, in "A Discussion of Margaret Atwood's *Bodily Harm*," published in a Danish journal, focuses on religion as no other critic has. Arguing that the novel works through the old dispensation to make way for the new, a "medieval spiritual journey" that makes of Griswold the dark woods and Toronto a vanity fair, she gives detailed readings of the twin islands, both named after saints, and concludes by suggesting that Atwood has replaced divine grace with luck.

In all of these discussions of *Bodily Harm*, encouragement to maintain a sense of the novel's ambiguities, its contradictions, its density seems most important. Those readings that stress complexity are surely more fruitful than those that reductively fit the novel into preordained patterns. It is surprising, however, that such a subversive novel has resulted in so little controversy among critics. Hutcheon objects briefly to Powe's attack; Tiffin takes Strauss to task. Elsewhere, critics often discuss the novel in a vacuum, restating what has already been described, reiterating conclusions established earlier. If nothing else, I hope that the review of criticism stressed by this series will lead to more general argument about Canadian fiction.

Reading of the Text

INTRODUCTION

My reading of *Bodily Harm* is indebted to the reviews and articles on which I have already commented. Together, they form a dense gloss for investigating this complex and important work. As I have already suggested, Margaret Atwood's many interviews also establish networks of significance for the novel. Some of these include the author's interpretations of the novel or give suggestions about contexts which shaped the novel's direction. Although an author's comments should not take precedence over other commentary, they can, as in Atwood's case, give information that, spread over time, keeps the novel vital. Many of the interviews also emphasize either directly or indirectly national preoccupations. To use words from *Bodily Harm*, through them, the "sweet Canadians" may see themselves reflected.

The task of reading major interviews has been made easier with the publication of Earl Ingersoll's *Margaret Atwood: Conversations*, which begins with Graeme Gibson's 1973 interview and concludes with Ingersoll's 1989 interview, devoted to the haunted *Cat's Eye*. Margaret Kaminski's 1975 interview, in which Atwood talked about mythologies and mirror-images, is probably the first in the collection to elucidate themes and images later used in *Bodily Harm*. I have already mentioned the 1976 Sandler interview, perhaps the most quoted of all Atwood's conversations. In it, the author emphasized her fascination with metamorphosis, described mazes as descents into an underworld of creative potential, and insisted that, for her, "it's axiomatic that art has its roots in social realities" (53), although she also argued that writing suffers if authors become activists. Also in 1976, Atwood told J.R. (Tim) Struthers that she was a "very visually oriented" (60) person, commented on the playfulness of writers, and admitted that she did not like to enter her fiction through direct authorial intrusion, as it was used in the nineteenth century. She told Joyce Carol Oates in 1978 that people think of women as more subjective and lacking in inventiveness than men, and admitted to the Australian Jim Davidson that she wanted to change people so that what they see becomes more authentic. Talking about obscurity in a 1978 interview with Karla Hammond, she insisted that her characters (the reference is to *Life Before Man*) were not concealing anything. Rather, she said, "it's just that the true story of their life is used as a defense" (108). In the 1979 Hammond interview referred to above, she compared her writing to a lens rather than a mirror, emphasizing the ways in which it magnifies and focuses issues, rather than merely reflecting them.

This last interview took place not long before Atwood began writing *Bodily Harm*, on May 21, 1980, at 10:22 p.m., according to notes in the archives. Her mind was on Latin America. When she talked to Fitzgerald and Crabbe in 1979, she stressed that she was a political writer, and insisted that it was necessary to be from a country like Canada, peripheral in many ways, to understand her position. In 1981, in an interview with Alan Twigg, she said, in reference to Canada, that being morally superior is easy when one is in a position of relative powerlessness. "Fear," she also argued, "can be a real motivating factor" (*For Openers* 224), for "if you're not aware of the fact that you may die, you're much less careful about other people" (226).

Thereafter, references specifically to *Bodily Harm* crop up sporadically. In a 1982 conversation with Jo Brans, Atwood mentioned showing the manuscript to a West Indian, and told Brans that she considered *Bodily Harm* "the most affirmative" (Ingersoll 148) of her novels up to that date. She pointed out that

> part of what the novel does is set our way of thinking. . . . We can afford to worry about our personal health and our fitness and our personal romances, and what we're eating, and whether we're fashionable, and whether we look good, and personal change and growth and all of those things we read about in women's magazines — that's in the forefront of our lives (148).

26

Clearly, *Bodily Harm* aims to question such perspectives. She also attempted to define politics: "Politics, for me, is everything that involves who gets to do what to whom" (149). She insisted that it "has to do with how people order their societies, to whom power is ascribed, who is considered to have power," and emphasized that "nobody's immune" (149). Very much inside the novel's world, she pointed out that neurophysiologists agree that reading is close to actual experience. This emphasis on a book's intrusiveness (and the political novel surely aims to be intrusive) should remind us that readers of *Bodily Harm* are, like Rennie, trapped within its spaces.

Two 1983 interviews focus on issues raised in *Bodily Harm*. In response to a question about the ending of the novel, Atwood assured Jan Castro that Rennie "was involved already. Whether she got out or not is open to question" (Vanspanckeren and Castro 221). She told Castro that the novel's two islands (Ste. Agathe and St. Antoine) were a condensed version of three Caribbean islands with which she was familiar, and insisted that "nobody can claim to have the absolute, whole, objective, total, complete truth" (232). In the other interview, with Beatrice Mendez-Egle, Atwood mentioned that a number of men had apparently liked *Bodily Harm* the best of her novels and, with tongue in cheek, claimed to have a "sneaking suspicion that the reason was that it had guns and wars in it" (Ingersoll 162). Referring to the writing of the novel, she admitted that, although she had been collecting characters, scenes, and images, it fell into place only when someone on a West Indian beach told her the story of her life.

Atwood's 1985 interview with Jennifer Meese also illuminates *Bodily Harm*. In it, the author underscored her changed attitudes toward the intermarriage of politics and art, reiterated her conviction that gender relationships were as political as human rights issues and, in response to Meese's question, "When you wrote *Bodily Harm*, did you have any conscious awareness of things like body as body, body as text, and body as body politic playing together in relation particularly to disease or dis-ease?" answered: "The body as a concept has always been a concern of mine. It's there in *Surfacing* as well. I think that people very much experience themselves through their bodies. . . . I'm interested in where you feel your body can go without being conspicuous or being put into danger" (187). Claiming that Americans are likely to think that free choice means that everything becomes a choice, she stressed that Canadians like herself tend to believe that human beings have a "limited smorgasbord" (189). She agreed with Meese that Rennie, helped to understand sexual commitment by reflecting on her mother and grandmother, "makes a very big move. She accepts responsibility for another human being, which this society does not encourage. This is a society of individuals" (190).

In the 1987 interview with Bonnie Lyons quoted above, Atwood made a comment that has profoundly affected my reading of the novel. Asked whether Rennie was an indivdual character or a representative everywoman, Atwood answered: "Why does it have to be either/or?" (Ingersoll 227). I want to reiterate Atwood's rejection of exclusive arguments, her preference for inclusive interpretations. *Bodily Harm* lends itself to multiple readings. Much of its density results from its positive ambivalence. The novel poses questions about power, about politics and art, about human bodies, and about women's friendships that have no concise answers. This novel illustrates many ways of seeing. As Atwood also said to Lyons, even the "sexual kink and violence" in the novel, read in certain ways in North America, would be read very differently in countries where sex is "a political instrument, an instrument of control. It's not something weird sadists and porn fanciers do; it's something governments do to people to keep them under control" (227). My reading, then, is particularly influenced by an awareness of multiplicity, and by the physical nature of the story.

Sometimes, I imagine *Bodily Harm* itself as a body, enclosing its readers, subjecting us to its wounds. Talking with me about the novel in 1991, Carolyn Forché described *Bodily Harm* as exemplary of how the political can be internalized, the internal politicized. According to her, in contradiction to the fascist impulse to eliminate the body, to take away the body's authority, Atwood has written a subversive novel, in which text and body are equated — a deeply threatening venture. Atwood has shown us, said Forché, that each of us must participate in the other's pain, that the dismembered body, as she and Atwood talked about it in the late 1970s, has come to represent political repression. The two writers agreed about the difficulties of reporting events taking place in Central America to a North American audience. In "Notes Toward a Poem That Can Never Be Written," which she dedicated to Forché, Atwood describes a place "you would rather not know about," a place that "will inhabit you" (TS 65). The poet talks about "sandpits" filled with bodies (66), about a woman "dying for the sake of the word," her body "silent / and fingerless" (67) writing the poem. She parallels torture and operations and tells her apparently Canadian audience that whether "bad dream[s]," "hallucination," or "vision," "Witness is what you must bear" (69). In *Bodily Harm*, Rennie Wilford bears witness.

DEDICATIONS AND EPIGRAPHS

Apart from dedicating *Bodily Harm* to Canadian writer Graeme Gibson, with whom she has lived since 1973, and his two sons, Atwood also dedicated this novel to the Australian poet Jennifer Rankin. Rankin died from breast cancer in 1979. This fact alone makes appropriate the dedication of a novel in which the main character suffers from breast cancer. But the dedication might also alert readers to a collection of Rankin's poetry, *Earth Hold*, published in 1978. While not openly political, many of Rankin's poems seem to suspend time and space in ways remarkably similar to moments of suspension in *Bodily Harm*. Here are the first four stanzas of "Island Crossing":

> I sailed to an island,
> It was not there.
>
> I flew in a plane from the mainland.
> It did not exist.
>
> I walked on countless coral reefs
> cutting my feet even my tongue bleeding
>
> and they were not to be seen.
> All these things existed and were not there. (4)

In this poem, Rankin uses contradiction to establish ambiguity. The island is there and not there; the plane flight occurs and does not occur. Such ambiguity evokes *Bodily Harm*'s surreal atmosphere. Throughout Rankin's poetry, images suggestively resonate: from

"Earth Count," "Now I speak a subterranean language / burrowing in beneath the ground" (29); from "Sand," "We are the space between the sea and others, / We sit on the beach telling stories" (40); from "Morning Tide," "I am lop-sided and uneven. / I am the funny figure in this mirror-maze" (47); from "Littorals," "This is blood / and an island of towered prison. / Here windows are thin slits in the body of stone" (52) and, from the same poem, "Marooned between zones I have been reminded" (55).

I have quoted from Rankin's poems, not because themes and images contained in them can explain *Bodily Harm*, but because they add another way of seeing the novel. So do early drafts of the novel. I have already pointed out the influence of John Berger's *Ways of Seeing*; a quotation from his book is the only epigraph used in the published *Bodily Harm*. But I did not mention the many quotations abandoned as epigraphs while Atwood came to her final decision. Originally titled "The Robber Bridegroom," referring to the Grimm's fairytale of that name, and then "Rope Quartet," a title that points to the rope in the novel's opening scene, early versions of the manuscript list many potential epigraphs (Box 33, Atwood Archives). They are variously revealing. An early quotation from "The Robber Bridegroom" evokes the uncanny atmosphere Atwood has created in *Bodily Harm*. It reads: "Then said the bridegroom to the bride: 'Come, my darling, do you know nothing? Relate something to us like the rest.' She replied: 'Then I will relate a dream.' "

Other abandoned epigraphs include quotations from Flannery O'Connor's letters ("The truth does not change according to our ability to stomach it emotionally"); from James Reaney's poem, "The School Globe," in which a child's pleasant world turns into one filled with "blood, pus, horror and death"; from Louise Bogan's "Journeys around My Room"; from Pablo Neruda's "The Heroes" ("This story is horrifying; if you have suffered from it, forgive me, but I'm not sorry"); from Thomas Rourke's *The Life of Vincent Gomez*, about "the type of men who could do these things to other men"; from Richard Seltzer's *Confessions of a Knife*, and another from his *Mortal Lessons*: "to search for some meaning in the ritual of surgery, which is at once murderous, powerful, healing and full of love"; from Hugh Drummond's "Diagnosing Marriage," from *Mother Jones* ("We have to see how issues of power invade every aspect of every relationship in a society that worships it"); from Miguel Algarin,

"What do I do when I am told a lie about events that have happened in my lifetime? I listen for stories"; from Eleanora Alcuin's *Parables*,

> I hope you are not innocent enough to believe that
> everything I say is true;
> I hope you are not innocent enough to believe that
> nothing I say is true.
> I hope you are not innocent enough to believe.
> I hope you are not innocent.
> Enough to believe.
> I hope;

a Peruvian proverb, "What you are willing to swallow depends on how hungry you are"; a comment by Quentin Bell on fashion; a quote from Isaak Dinessen, "Men and women are two locked caskets, each bearing within it the key to the other"; and, finally, one from T.S. Eliot, "Every man wants to, needs to, has to / Sometimes, somewhere, do a girl in."

These abandoned potential epigraphs maintain emotional and intellectual associations in the finished version of *Bodily Harm*. Like Jennifer Rankin's poetry, they act as particles in the charged field of energy out of which the novel emerged. They affected my re-readings and gave resonance to some of my speculations. I wondered if the novel had originally been conceived as a dream, as the quotation from "The Robber Bridegroom" suggests, and as many of Rankin's poems appear to be. We can see how the quotations gloss the novel's major themes: power; punishment; torture; the status of truth and the "real"; stories; surgery; lies; innocence; hunger; clothes; caskets and so on. They open up *Bodily Harm*.

PART ONE (INVISIBILITY)

The manuscripts also reveal tentative beginnings for the novel (Boxes 33 and 34, Atwood Archives). What emerged as the first sentence, "This is how I got here, says Rennie" (11),[1] might have been, "I'm still alive, that's something"; or "This is why I left (said Rennie)"; or "This was the beginning of it"; or "This is how I got here"; or "This was the second thing." Several of these sentences give plot information or temporal sequence that the author rejected. It seems correct, then, to emphasize the ambiguity of *Bodily Harm*'s first sentence and to underline its unsettling emphasis on a time and space that the reader initially cannot straighten out.

Following the opening sentence, which is separated from the subsequent paragraph and different in verb tense, Rennie begins to describe her return from a shopping trip and her discovery of two policemen in the apartment she had shared with Jake. At first, she thought they were looking for drugs, but in fact they were investigating a break-in. The intruder had left a coiled rope on Rennie's bed. This allusion to the game of Clue is underlined by Rennie as she vaguely recalls the game's rules: "You had to guess three things: Mr. Green, in the conservatory, with a pipewrench; Miss Plum, in the kitchen, with a knife" (13). This recollected scene establishes what will become the novel's obsession with policemen, with violence, and with intrusions into female space. It also gives the reader "clues" to the novel's direction. Throughout, the questions who? where? with what?, sometimes asked directly, sometimes only by implication, crop up with surprising frequency. Are we meant to think of *Bodily Harm* as a game? Do correct answers exist for its various configurations of weapons, rooms, and suspects?

But just as the reader begins to settle into Rennie's story, the novel breaks off, shifting into the third person and the present tense. The break is marked by a small, circular, black dot, visually striking, a large period. In earlier drafts, the sections are separated by an intricate, flower-like design, suggestive of the fleur-de-lis, and Atwood's change of design implies a desire to simplify, perhaps to shock. Following the dot, the narrator (we are now being told *about* Rennie) describes Rennie, who is in an airport in the Barbados where her plane to the Caribbean has briefly stopped. She wears a dress of "washed-out blue" (15), a neutral color, almost invisible. We are assured that she is lucky. *Visor*, the magazine for which she writes, has agreed to send her to an out-of-the-way island in order to do a travel piece. The decision was sudden. Rennie is therefore flying "blind," not having had time to learn about the island in advance. In the airport, she nurses a gin and tonic, and looks at the shops.

Another break in the narrative occurs, this time so that the narrator can fill us in on some of Rennie's background. She comes from the Canadian town of Griswold, where people seem to be boring and judgemental, never on the side of the victim, convinced that people deserve to have bad things happen to them. This disturbing information, apparently connected to Rennie's response to the episode of the rope on the bed, triggers other recent bits of information. We find out that Rennie has had an operation for breast cancer, that she is an "expert on boredom" (19), that she has worked for a publication called *Pandora* (even the most literal reader will note this allusion carefully), and that her relationship with Jake has been a difficult one.

Let me pause in this somewhat pedestrian report of the novel's development. Although the novel's sequence matters, the impression given by the novel is hardly reproduced in my summary. For one thing, the tone of both first-person and third-person sections is similarly cold and the distances between the narrator and the characters and the readers, carefully maintained. More difficult to locate, an eery, dream-like quality embues both past and present. At the end of the section on Rennie's background, we are told that, during love-making with Jake, Rennie's "body was nerveless, slack" and that Jake seemed to be "trying to break through that barrier of deadened flesh" (21). This sinister description verges on hysteria.

And so the first section of the novel proceeds, jumping back and forth between episodes from the past, not chronologically arranged, about Rennie's operation and about Jake's moving out of the apartment, to present events which occur in chronological order. Rennie boards the airplane, now on its way to the Caribbean, thinks about her operation and about Dr. Daniel Luoma, the surgeon who performed it and with whom she believes herself to be in love, and reflects on conversations about trends with her Toronto friend, Jocasta, another strikingly suggestive name. We learn that Rennie's style of journalism focuses on catchy, superficial topics. Once seated in the airplane, Rennie discovers her seat-mate to be a veterinarian educated in Canada. Dr. Minnow, for that is his name, subjects Rennie to a series of ironic comments about the "sweet Canadians" (29), an expression that forms a certain recitative throughout the novel. Defensive about her reasons for visiting the Caribbean, Rennie appears anxious as she steps out of the plane, and thinks of herself as "invisible" (39) in the taxi she takes into town. In the dining room of the motel where she will stay, Rennie sees a woman with "fluorescent teeth" and "blue china-doll eyes" (42), and has a snappy, flirtatious conversation with a man called Paul. We are given detailed information about the restaurant's food: *"the local bread, and butter of perhaps questionable freshness"*; the badly cooked roast beef; the "cube of yam"; the "something light green that has been boiled too long"; the "whipped lime Jello" (42–43). Some of this information, presented in italics, represents the kind of journalistic reporting done by Rennie, and some, given to us by the narrator, echoes Rennie's speech. The specificity of detail seems slightly peculiar. As in many other places in the novel, the often abrupt shifts between careful observation, given under the narrator's apparently meticulous control, and a bewildering unfocussed vagueness that leaves the reader abandoned, increase anxiety.

The last of the eleven segments that make up Part One takes place in Rennie's room at the motel, the Sunset Inn. Again, the reader is given much specific detail ranging from descriptions of the floral, pink-and-blue wallpaper, to the picture of an opened, green melon, to the mermaid lamp, "with her arms over her head, holding up the bulb. Her breasts aren't bare, she's wearing a harem jacket open at the front, its edges grazing the nipples" (47). We are guided through Rennie's nightly ablutions, and watch her get into bed. Then, in a four-paragraph conclusion, the narrator compounds the images that have been accumulating throughout the section. Described as floating in a suspended state, Rennie shifts between sleep and wakefulness. At one point, jolted into consciousness, she feels the mosquito net pressing down on her face, and sees the dot of her digital clock "pulsing" like a "tiny heart" (49). She has been dreaming about an anonymous intruder, and has the uneasy feeling that she may have been screaming. Outside, she hears a rooster crowing, a dog barking. And, in an adjoining room, she hears a woman, her voice "wordless and mindless" (49), apparently in the act of copulation.

The intensity of this concluding segment results partly from its evocation of stifling suffocation (the oppressive heat, the small room, the clinging mosquito net), and partly from the use of words like "agony," "painful," and "severed." It projects anxiety and even a tightly controlled terror that seem to have no immediate cause but that make the reader uneasy. The narrative's duplicity, up to now evidenced mainly in its split time and narrative voice, now also suggests secrecy. The concluding italicized *"Oh please,"* which comes at us from an unnamed space and is spoken by an unknown voice, returns us to the novel's opening, to the ambiguity of time and space.

34

Although a number of markers exist throughout the section, we still do not know exactly where we are, or when.

So it is that this story makes readers uneasy. Our uneasiness is exacerbated by references to intrusion. Rennie's personal space, her apartment, as if it were an extension of her body, has been invaded, first by the anonymous intruder, and then by the two threatening policemen. As they look at Rennie, and at the objects in her apartment, they try to control them. Film theory tells us much about the intrusive gaze, and Rennie admits that the invader has made her aware of being seen "too intimately, her face blurred and distorted, damaged, owned in some way she couldn't define" (40). Even her memories prove intrusive. We are told that she has attempted to put Griswold behind her, but that she finds it impossible to rid herself of the town's moral judgements, its relish in blaming the victim. As the novel progresses, the reader will hear more of the effects of the past on the present, and will discover repeated parallels between Rennie's sense of physical violation and the guilt she carries with her from the past. Like the present, the past also inflicts harm.

Descriptions of physical intrusions elicit corresponding responses from readers. Rennie's relationship with Jake is described as a campaign to "alter her" (15). Wanting her to become an extension of his own sexual fantasies, Jake buys her "garters, merry widows, red bikini pants with gold spangles, wired half-cup hooker brassieres that squeezed and pushed up the breasts." A continued relationship, she imagines, would have led to "black leather and whips" (20). Jake intrudes on Rennie's space. Their lovemaking seems pathological as Jake wrenches, twists, bites; Rennie remains inert, a "barrier of deadened flesh" (21). She recalls how Jake's lunchtime surprises obscenely parody sexual molesters as he comes through the apartment window rather than the door.

But the most visceral images of bodily harm coalesce around Rennie's operation. On almost every page, the reader is reminded of breasts, of cancer, of death. We feel Rennie's aching left shoulder, her obsession with knives and teeth (Jake's "long canines" [15], for example), her persistent awareness of a wound and her repeated analyses of her physical condition. Before the operation, she imagined her body as "permeated, riddled, rotting away from the inside" (19); after, she exposes her damaged breast to the policemen and, as she climbs into the airplane that will take her to the Caribbean, "she's afraid she'll see blood, leakage, her stuffing coming out" (22). She thinks of publicity as baring one's throat to the knife (26), and falling in love with one's doctor as part of a "sex-and-scalpel" epic (33). The word *"Malignant"* (32), with its reference to spreading cancer cells, crops up intermittently, like a blip on a computer screen, and the expression "massive involvement" (34) forewarns of destruction. The picture of the opened melon, the mermaid lamp with its partially exposed breasts, and the equation between tooth decay and cancer, set the scene for the last section of Part One. Rennie lies in bed, her "left hand on her right breast, right hand on the ridge of skin that slants across the side of the breast up towards the armpit" (48). We are forced to pay attention to broken and wounded bodies. Rennie wonders what happens to cut-off body parts following operations, and imagines herself being buried "one piece at a time" (23). She thinks of newspaper stories about women's bodies, broken and scattered in ravines.

Part One also begins to construct tensions between surfaces and depths that will recur throughout the novel. Cutting through skin to reveal the hidden disease beneath becomes visually and metaphorically the central theme of *Bodily Harm*. The novel stresses many superficialities. For example, Rennie initially rejects a serious literary career, preferring to record other people's statements so that she can remain neutral and invisible, "off to the side" (26). Concerned mainly with appearances, she avoids probing into underlying economic and political problems, and makes sure that the *Visor* editor will not expect from her any analysis of Caribbean politics. She willfully misses Dr. Minnow's irony as he talks about the "sweet Canadians" (29), repeating that she is simply writing a "travel piece" (29), a genre she assumes will exclude her from massive involvement. Although she begins to feel "very white" among the black faces of the island, she tells herself that she is "safe" (39). Thus, Rennie struggles to skim life's surfaces, while the reader, gleaning troubling psychological, moral, and political information, recognizes cover-ups and rationalizations. Tension. We learn that the Canadians have donated one thousand tins of ham to the government of St. Antoine following a devastating hurricane, but that the refugees have not received them. Dr. Minnow contrasts British imperialism with the "broken pots" (30) made by the native Caribs, and points out that the originally British Fort George has been renamed Fort Industry. He describes his ineffective efforts to lengthen the island's dangerously short runway and, as they disembark, tells Rennie that although he comes from a family of pirates, many of the members have become respectable by marrying with the British. As usual, Rennie misses the irony.

While it emphasizes surfaces, *Bodily Harm* involves itself in depth. Comparisons between the final version of the novel and earlier manuscript versions make clear that Atwood has held back information. In an early typescript, the woman Rennie meets in the motel's dining room (later revealed as Lora), speaks near the beginning of the novel, telling us that she and Rennie are in a jail cell. She says: "We're sitting on this tropical island, with these palm trees and a full moon, just like in the movies, only there happens to be this wall, and outside of it people are getting killed maybe" (Box 33, Atwood Archives, 30). Atwood's decision to remove this passage and to save the jail cell references for Part Six indicates a desire to confuse. The drafts also emphasize the significance of Rennie's conviction, faced with Daniel's dualistic thinking, that choices ought to be multiple rather than "[e]ither/or" (23). Part One invites multiple readings. Massive involvement applies to political bodies, to the cancer-ridden body of the novel's main character, and to the many levels of meaning that make up the body of the text. So do invisibility, and the cutting open of surfaces to expose hidden material. Time and space, inside and outside, peculiarly intertwine, reverse, and alternate. Shadows replace substantial structures; we are denied firm footing anywhere.

PART TWO (SILENCE)

Part Two also begins in Rennie's voice and again, we do not know who listens to her remarks. She talks about her past; rather than the narrator's abrupt and distanced summary of the past's intrusions into Rennie's present, we have Rennie's own sensual evocation of her grandmother's house. She recalls "weak yellowish winter light" (53) coming through a bedroom window and the silence and chill of the cell-like cellar, with its "single light bulb" (53). She tells us about her grandfather, a country doctor. From her grandmother's stories, Rennie imagined him to be a hero, a man who drove through blizzards to "tear babies out through holes he cut in women's

37

stomachs," who "amputated a man's leg with an ordinary saw," and who risked his life when he entered a house where a crazy man who had "blown the head off one of his children" (55) threatened to shoot him. Her mother and aunts have told Rennie less heroic stories about their father's bad temper, but these, like the grandmother's stories, were difficult for Rennie to connect with the "frail old man" (56) whom she knew as her grandfather. These multiple and contradictory stories emphasize gender, physical transformations, and alternative ways of seeing.

Stressing intrusion, and scattered pieces of bodies, Part Two describes bodily harm in the past, as well as the present. Rennie recalls her grandmother's deterioration; the old woman had first lost her balance, and then her memory. With considerable poignancy, the granddaughter recalls the grandmother's search for the hands she imagined she had lost: "My hands, she said. I've left them somewhere and now I can't find them" (57). This emphasis on hands reflects similar references in Part One. Emerging from the anesthetic following her operation, Rennie watches the doctor's hand as if it were an isolated part of his body, until it "attached itself to his arm" (32) Later, she looks at Paul's hands which she describes as "square-fingered and practical, carpenter's hands" (46). In Part Two, she speaks of her grandmother looking for her "other hands, the ones I had before, the ones I touch things with" (57), and we begin to understand that, in her grandmother's plight, Rennie sees her own. Like her grandmother, she has become distanced from her body, unable to touch others. The image has religious overtones.

The novel now jumps to a series of scenes that apparently take place on the island of St. Antoine. Dressed in a "plain white cotton dress," Rennie gets ready to go out. As she performs various actions, she contemplates the meaning of *"terminal,"* (59) and describes again her sense of suspension, as if she were experiencing a "half-life" (60) between living and dying. The narrator conjures up a vivid sense of imminent physical harm as Rennie describes a dream in which "the scar on her breast splits open like a diseased fruit" (60) and a venomous creature crawls out: one of the horrors of the half-lived life. Then, in the motel's dining-room, Rennie rehearses her "story," the one she is supposed to be writing for *Visor*. This rehearsal allows the narrator, through Rennie, to make observations about the nature of narrative in the post-modern age. These revolve around tensions between surfaces and depths, fiction and reality. Rennie claims that she no longer believes in "real" stories, or concerns herself with "issues" (64). Style wins out over content, trends over substance. This attention to fictionality marks *Bodily Harm* throughout.

Once out on one of St. Antoine's streets, Rennie carefully avoids looking at the more troubling aspects of the island. She goes into a drugstore and, in another of the novel's frequent references to drugs, the druggist asks her if she wants " 'the hard stuff' " (69). Inside a church, Rennie sees a painting of a black St. Anthony being tempted in a desert filled oddly with "vivid succulent red flowers" (70) and recalls a trip to Mexico with Jake. While there, she saw Virgins whose skirts "had been studded with little tin images" (70) that, on closer inspection, often turned out to be parts of bodies that needed to be healed. Now, the custom attracts Rennie; she can imagine pinning parts of herself to the Virgin's skirt. Her recollections of Mexico increase her tendency to distance herself from the native people. There, as she has up to this point in St. Antoine, she behaved as a tourist. From the church, Rennie walks towards the harbour and, for the first time since she has arrived, one of the native islanders touches her, a black, somewhat shrunken man, his fly partly undone, his feet bare — the man she had stepped over earlier. As he tries to get her attention, Rennie panics; the reader also succumbs to the suspicions and underlying fears built up in Part One as female bodies suffer from various attacks. But here, Rennie's terror proves, at least temporarily, unfounded. Paul intervenes, explaining that the old man, who is deaf and dumb, merely wants to bring Rennie good luck. "Reluctantly," Rennie puts her hand into the old man's and, because of this action and Paul's presence, feels, for a moment, as if she has been "rescued" (75).

Throughout this series of events, the narrator follows Rennie as if viewing her through the lens of a camera. We also have the sense of being shown specific actions that will change Rennie from being a tourist into being someone who pays close attention to the world around her. We understand that she will be unable to remain closed. The touch of the deaf and dumb man represents a different kind of interference from that described earlier. The novel now reveals alternative ways of opening the body and different reasons for the bodily harm on which it has concentrated. Some of these have religious implications. For example, the laying on of hands often precedes religious conversion. Christ's words to the disciples at the last supper are echoed: "This is my body, which is given for you" (Luke 22:19). The introduction of a character called the "Prince of Peace" should come as no surprise. We find out shortly that Prince, directed by a man called Marsdon, is running in the first local election since the departure of the British, as an "excuse for communists" (77), against Dr. Minnow who, like Prince, wants Ste. Agathe to separate from St. Antoine. Both islands are currently run by Ellis. As if to give substance to the rumors Rennie has heard about Caribbean hostility to visitors, Marsdon warns Rennie to leave the island, but Paul assures her that, although there will be trouble, her tourist status makes her "exempt" (78).

This attention to island politics reminds us of Rennie's discussions with Dr. Minnow on the plane. Although now, as then, she is unable to take what she imagines to be small-time political problems seriously, the narrator gives us signals that should forewarn us. One of Ellis's posters has been "defaced with red paint" (70); Marsdon wears boots, the first Rennie has seen on the islands; a man wearing "a white shirt and mirror sunglasses" (78) barks at a crowd through a bullhorn; people respond by throwing objects at the truck. Atwood took particular care with her descriptions of the island's political climate. The West Indian she had read the manuscript responded with detailed information about forts, telling Atwood that only one West Indian island has a fort, and remarked, apropos of drugs, that "Ellis doesn't want the peasants growing the stuff and marketing it themselves. He'll get no cut out of that. He's got to keep the trade" (Box 37, Atwood Archives).

After lunch, Rennie wanders down to the beach where, bored, she watches three men "cutting the heads off fish, gutting them and tossing them into a red plastic pail" (79). Similar images, situated differently and with various functions, recur throughout the rest of the novel. Rennie continues along the beach, buys a ticket to take *The Princess Anne* to another island (the name of the other boat, *The Princess Margaret*, emphasizes recent British colonization) and, while waiting to board, experiences the by-now expected sensation of her amorphous physical boundaries: "her real fear, irrational but a fear, is that the scar will come undone in the water, split open like a faulty zipper, and she will turn inside out" (80). Slit fish, broken bodies, cuts, and forced entrances condense, as obsessive as images in dreams, possible clues to help put together a story. We are reminded to wonder about what is happening to whom, and where. As she waits for the boat, Rennie also thinks about her mother, and then of her doctor, Daniel. Before she had left Canada, she told him that she did not feel "human any more," but full of "white maggots" (83) that seemed to be eating her insides away.

Once on the boat, the woman Rennie had noticed in the dining room the night before joins her. Ominously introduced as a "darker shadow" (85), she repels Rennie, mainly because her "fingers holding the cigarette are bitten to the quick, stub-tipped, slightly grubby, the raw skin around the nails nibbled as if mice have been at them" (86). Rennie admits that "she doesn't like the sight of ravage, damage, the edge between inside and outside blurred like that" (86). The suspicious words here, "gnawed," "ravage," and "damage," and the emphasis on the blurring of "the edge between inside and outside," vividly reflect Rennie's own bodily harm, her sense of having lost her shape, her belief that her boundaries are dissolving. They imply unclear distinctions among the political parties that have just been described. They also alert us to the difficulties of reading *Bodily Harm*. Because the narrative boundaries are fluid, readers cannot be sure when they are inside someone's perspective, and when outside. The shifts between first-person and third-person narration actively participate in this confusion.

When Lora introduces herself to Rennie, she makes a point of spelling her name which, in manuscript versions, is spelled Laura. This change, one of several name changes, reminds us that Atwood places great importance on the names of her characters and tempts us to associate this name with, for example, the word "oral." Like almost everyone else in the novel, when she begins to speak, Lora describes bodily harm: " 'A girl I know, she woke up in the middle of the night and there was this black guy in a bathing suit holding a knife to her throat' " (86) and, as if repeating the novel's opening scene, implies that the attacker may have been a policeman. Together, Lora and Rennie wade out to the boat and, sitting on the boat's bench, the exhaust blowing into her face, Rennie tries to concentrate on her surroundings. She still plans to write about them. But when Lora suggests that Rennie should write about Lora's life, Rennie becomes "instantly bored" (89) and wonders, as she has before, why people want so much to be *"seen"* (89). This observation reminds us of

Rennie's earlier insistence on the advantages of invisibility and allows her to return to another unsettling image: "Rennie switches off the sound and concentrates only on the picture" (89). This desire to watch rather than to experience, as if what were happening were flat image rather than multi-dimensional life, again reminds us of the duplicities of the novel. Apart from underlining the fact that *Bodily Harm* emphasizes many ways of seeing, the emphasis on watching also tells us that confusions between inside and outside continue, and that subjectivity and objectivity, fiction and life, text and body cannot be clearly separated. Rennie's interest in making Lora over recalls Jake's efforts to reconstruct Rennie. Now Rennie too intrudes on a woman's space.

The scene jumps — we are surely by now accustomed to the abrupt shifts of locale in this novel — to the patio of St. Antoine's Driftwood Hotel. The narrator draws attention to the racial mix; white people and one Indian family seated, while black and brown people serve them. Again, huge red flowers surround the scene and what is becoming a common aural effect, the sound of buzzing or humming, reverberates from the hummingbirds in the blossoms. These repetitions of visual and aural imagery encourage readers to search for clues to establish the space and time of the novel. Another scene, imagined but not enacted, recalls an earlier one. In response to Lora's aggressiveness, Rennie thinks about exposing her damaged breast, as she had earlier exposed it to the policemen in her Toronto apartment. Thus, bodily harm confirms Rennie in her role as victim.

Further references to drugs pick up again a major theme. Lora shuffles in her purse, pulls out a bag of grass and offers some to Rennie. Although Rennie, somewhat self-righteously, refuses, she is horrified when two policemen saunter over to the table. These men are selling tickets to the Policeman's Ball, but their appearance propels Lora into a general diatribe against the island's policemen. She says that they misuse their power, particularly against women: " 'Then they use your first name. Not Miss or Mrs. or anything, your first name, and you've got no way of knowing any of their names at all' " (93). As Lora talks, Rennie becomes increasingly dizzy from alcohol. Throughout the novel, often portrayed as confused, disoriented, slightly drugged, or drunk, Rennie may see nothing clearly at all. We also question her judgement. She has accepted and transcribed reports that women are deceitful and "difficult to work with," while men put everything "out on the table." Her editor, a man, has congratulated her on her *perception* (93).

Following some brief observations about exchanging sex for police favours, and after a conversation with Paul who has suddenly reappeared, Lora asks Rennie to do her a favour by picking up a box from New York, to be delivered to the airport the following day. According to Lora, it contains heart medicine for Elva, an old woman who lives on St. Antoine's twin island of Ste. Agathe, and is the mother of Lora's current boyfriend, the political candidate, Prince. By now quite drunk, Rennie accepts the customs slip. Paul drives her back to the Sunset Inn, but on the way, she gets out of the jeep to be sick and, as if the author were flirting with the formula for a Harlequin romance, Paul kisses her. At her request, he has taken off the mirror sunglasses which made him appear "faceless" (99). The setting, however, is not romantic. Rennie has noticed rotting coconuts and burrows made by the landcrabs, both of which remind her of her damaged breast and discourage her from letting Paul enter her motel room. Once alone, the effects of alcohol somewhat dissipated, Rennie lights up one of the joints Lora has given her. Almost immediately, she enters a transition state, in which she thinks about the darkly dividing cells of her body and about her relationship with her ex-lover, Jake.

Memories of this relationship take us to the end of Part Two. Rennie admits that by the time she had met Jake, "she'd decided she didn't much like being in love," and constructs a startling, although in terms of this novel, appropriate simile: "being in love was like running barefoot along a street covered with broken bottles" (102). In other words, Rennie assumes love to be conducive to bodily harm. The photographer who took Jake's picture for the story Rennie was writing when she met Jake called Jake a "prick" (103), and condescendingly acknowledged that women prefer men who treat them badly. Rennie did not argue. Rather, she defended Jake's competence. A designer, a packager, Jake "decided how things would look and what contexts they would be placed in, which meant what people would feel about them" (103). And because he understood contexts, Jake placed Rennie easily. He knew that she was not looking for a deep relationhsip and he responded to her superficially. With her, he could continue to do what he was good at: packaging. Ambiguously responding to his control, Rennie recalls having said: "Sometimes I feel like a blank sheet of paper. . . . For you to doodle on," although

Jake, also ambiguously and forebodingly, assured her that it was "all there underneath" (105).

Jake had also decorated their apartment. In the livingroom, he hung photographs of three Mexican prostitutes; in the bedroom, "a Heather Cooper poster, a brown-skinned woman wound up in a piece of material that held her arms to her sides but left her breasts and thighs and buttocks exposed. She had no expression on her face, she was just standing there" (105). The other bedroom picture features a woman lying "feet-first, and her head, up at the other end of the sofa, was tiny, featureless, and rounded like a doorknob. In the foreground there was a bull" (105–06). These pictures caused the policemen, at the beginning of Part One, to question Rennie, "grinning" (14), and they reflect the Berger epigraph that a "woman's presence . . . defines what can and cannot be done to her." Now, thinking about Jake from a different perspective, Rennie admits that the pictures made her nervous. She changes the romantic words that Jake probably did not say, "I want to be the one you open up for," to the more threatening and likely words, "I want to be the one who opens you up" (106). Thus, as Part Two concludes, we are thrown back into the scenario of Rennie's operation, where intrusion and cutting remain dominant sensations.

In Part One, closed spaces govern the different settings. Like Rennie, we feel trapped in the invaded apartment, the almost suffocating cabin of the airplane, the women's washroom and the restaurant in the Barbados airport, the hospital room, the terminal in St. Antoine, the "marshmallow-soft upholstery" (38) of the taxi Rennie takes to the motel, the motel's diningroom and, finally, the motel's bedroom, with its "single and narrow" (47) bed. The whole of Part One concentrates, almost obsessively, on interior spaces.

In Part Two, interior and exterior spaces alternate with each other, although we never really get away from suggestions of claustrophobia and suffocation. Interior spaces, like the grandmother's threatening cellar, even her whole house to which Rennie's mother and aunts were not given keys, dominate Rennie's memories of her childhood. Now, on the island of St. Antoine, which is itself a cut-off place, small and surrounded by water, Rennie continues to feel suffocated by the rather grubby motel and the hostile British woman who runs it. The church she visits is enclosed by a graveyard, and it reminds Rennie of Jake's statement about women: "You should all be locked in cages"

(73). On the boat, Rennie feels trapped by Lora, as she also does on the battered truck that takes her and Lora to the Driftwood. Paul's jeep is open-sided, but even in it, Rennie feels sick. As the first section did, this too ends with Rennie enclosed in her motel bedroom, alone.

Even when she is outside, wandering in the town's maze-like streets, or being chased through them, Rennie does not feel free. Nor is the reader allowed to relax. Harm lurks around every corner. Only one open space described in this section seems positive, although even by Rennie's childhood, it too had deteriorated and represents, therefore, a longed for, rather than an experienced, space. It is Rennie's grandmother's garden: "Once it had been filled with flowers, zinnias and scarlet runner beans on poles where the hummingbirds would come" (58). Rennie associates this space with heaven, and its decayed state with her fallen and diseased condition. That the motel's restaurant in St. Antoine has no fresh fruit suggests, too, a fall from Eden. The church's vine-covered gravestones seem more wasteland than garden, and when Rennie recollects the park that she and Jake visited in Mexico, she remembers most clearly a sign that, like one of the signs so significant to Malcolm Lowry's consul in *Under the Volcano*, seems to have been incorrectly translated: "*Those found sitting improperly in the park will be punished by the authorities*" (71).[2] The market, in the amorphously shaped town square, is crowded and noisy and, at the storefront cafe to which Paul leads her, Rennie sits next to the wall. At the Driftwood, she sits with Lora under a metal umbrella and, when she gets out of Paul's jeep, hears "birds, thin shrill voices like fingernails, raucous croaks, insects" (99). These are not comforting natural images. Even the quite positive hummingbirds of her grandmother's garden, more ominously "swarm" (90) on this island.

Other image patterns stand out. We learn more about Rennie's family, and the spaces of her family home parallel more recent spaces. More than in Part One, suggestions of vertical movement distract us from the horizontal direction of our reading. Descriptions of subterranean spaces proliferate, and we recognize what many critics have pointed out, that these may well represent the initial stage on Rennie's journey toward rebirth. In *Bodily Harm*, they also exaggerate the persistent uncanniness of the invisible and suggest the physical betrayals of the hidden cancer. Rennie never forgets what is happening to her body. As a result, the way she sees, and even what she sees, reflect her awareness that what is going on under surfaces means more than what happens on top. Tension between the superficial and the profound affects Rennie's actions in the present, and defines the subjects that she dwells on from her past. In this novel, decay certainly functions as metaphor. We understand that it affects the body politic. But it is also a physical fact. Like many women in the actual world (Jennifer Rankin, for example), Rennie suffers from breast cancer and readers of this novel are not allowed to forget what it feels like to be inside a body as it copes with this illness.

The uneasiness that results from our experience of Rennie's ordeal often occurs because of the images and descriptions used. At the beginning of Part Two, Rennie vividly recalls the cold air in her grandmother's cellar, and the freezing cement floor. When she talks about relationships among members of her family, she emphasizes the oppressive silence that dominated their lives. Even the objects of the house, the "clocks, vases, end-tables, cabinets, figurines, cruet sets, cranberry glasses, china plates" (54) seemed weighted down with a choking density. They were collected, Rennie recalls, not for their beauty, but because they represented "decency" (54). Like these objects, female bodies were expected to be decent. Touching was not encouraged; it might interfere with the boundaries established by decency. Rennie was taught that "open" bodies were loose bodies, and women were certainly not encouraged to be loose.

As in Part One, images of physical harm recur throughout Part Two. Rennie dwells on her grandfather's relationship with his patients. What she remembers are those episodes that seem to reflect her own physical condition. She tells us that he opened up women's bodies, removed a man's leg, and dealt with a man who had shot off a child's head: violence. Her mother and aunts were afraid of their father; he had threatened to horsewhip them. But Rennie does not focus only on external violence and forcefully broken bodies. Her own consciousness of frailty makes her particularly sensitive to the body's decay. Thus, she speaks of her grandfather's aging, of her grandmother's loss of control, of her mother's "caved face" (58), and the pouches under the eyes of the female judge she was to have interviewed for *Pandora*. This attention occurs also in the present. Rennie imagines Lora's bitten fingernails to be signs of physical disintegration. She admits that she "used to pray that I wouldn't live long enough to get like my grandmother," and adds, ominously, "and now I guess I won't" (58). Although the ghostly inhabitant (the ovaltine-drinking intruder?) whom she imagines taking up residence in her Toronto apartment during her absence "wouldn't be eating" (59), she has left food in the refrigerator. Decaying food joins the images of deterioration suggested by the gutted fish, the aging copies of *Time* and *Newsweek*, and the "mottled plant" (61) in the lounge of the Sunset Inn. Even the name of the motel reminds us that all life leads to death.

Death is further emphasized as Rennie recalls her recent operation. In order to come to St. Antoine, she has missed a doctor's appointment, and although her escape means that she will not have to listen to the results of tests that were not taken, she cannot get her mind off what would probably have been discovered. Chillingly, she meditates on the words "remission" and "terminal," the latter eerily echoing her experiences in airports. To remind us of what must be faced by cancer patients, she lists "pain and deathly sickness, the cells bombarded, the skin gone antiseptic, the hair falling out" (59–60). As many patients do, she imagines searching for miracle cures: "the laying on of hands by those who say they can see vibrations flowing out of their fingers in the form of holy red light" (60). These hands, like others in this novel, image healing.

The novel's uncanniness also results from the frequent evocation of states of suspension. St. Antoine's heat threatens to make Rennie "comatose," "demoralized" (63), and she imagines herself in a Somerset Maugham novel (*The Quiet American?*) being carried around in a hammock. She wanders around the town, disoriented. When the deaf and dumb man touches her she feels "bewildered and threatened" (74), and imagines that someone is trying to steal her passport. Without it, she would be a person without a territory. Not for the first time, she imagines herself in the middle of a bad dream. Such "alien reaction paranoia" (76), Paul explains to her, sometimes results because she misreads signs. Some of these signs, "Ellis is King," "Prince of Peace," "The Fish Lives," are confusing, for although they apparently refer to politicians running in the island's forthcoming election, they are also the kind of slogans displayed by churches and religious hospitals. As she sits with Lora on the patio of the Driftwood, Rennie has several daquiris; the alcohol increases her disorientation. Later, she smokes dope and, lying on her bed at the Sunset Inn, concentrates on her "cells, whispering, dividing in darkness,

47

replacing each other one at a time; and of the other cells, the evil ones which may or may not be there, working away in her with furious energy, like yeast" (100). It seems odd that Rennie should always be represented in semi-conscious states.

Images of photography frequently crop up in this section, emphasizing the importance of seeing, but also underlining the effects of silence. Sometimes, the images play out the tension between looking and touching; at other times, as the difference between photography and radiology makes clear, they emphasize the contrast between superficial appearances and interior x-rays. These two ways of taking pictures tell very different stories. Rennie comes to think of photography as fake, for example when she imagines concocting an article on St. Antoine, opposing old and new worlds, and throwing in "a few photos from the lesser-known corners" of St. Kitts, another island entirely. She remembers to take her camera with her as she wanders around St. Antoine, even though, she admits, she is not a particularly good photographer. On a tourist brochure, she sees the photograph of a woman in a bathing suit with a black man beside her and, behind him, a machete. Rennie contrasts the beach she visits, which is "narrow and gravelly and dotted with lumps of coagulated oil" (79) with the iridescent, jewel-like beach on the brochure, and contemplates taking a more "realistic" picture of the men gutting the fish for the brochure. In the Church of St. Antoine, she picks up three postcards on which are pictures of a painting on the church's west wall. When she gets on the boat, she sees that an older couple are looking at birds through binoculars, and Rennie herself stares at underwater fish through the boat's glass. Thinking in terms of pictures, she imagines turning Lora from a living, talking person, into a silent image. A static Lora could be rearranged, becoming for Rennie a "makeover piece, before and after, with a series of shots in between showing the process" (89). In Paul's mirror sunglasses, Rennie can see "two little faces, white and tiny, reflected back at her" (99), and at the end of Part Two, she thinks about the *Visor* photographer who accompanied her to interview Jake, and about Jake's collection of photographs and pictures.

These images, whether still photographs or moving images with the sound turned off, suggest that the events of Part Two take place in an eery silence. Mostly, people do not communicate with each other easily. Rennie tells us that "as a child I learned three things well:

48

how to be quiet, what not to say, and how to look at things without touching them." In Griswold, "the silences were almost visible" (54). On the island, the deaf and dumb man becomes a symbol of the various political silences and secrets that, like Rennie's cells, are "dividing in darkness," "working away" with "furious energy" (100).

PART THREE (DIS/EASE)

As Part Three opens, we again hear Rennie's voice. Now, she describes her father, and tells us that he had left home when she was a child. Because he returned to Griswold every Christmas to keep up appearances, Rennie did not understand that her parents were actually separated. When she was thirteen, and beginning to menstruate, her mother told her of the divorce. Such equivocation marks many of Rennie's relationships. Rennie also emphasizes the importance of space. While she was attending university in Toronto, she visited her father and his wife, and discovered that, although they lived in an apartment considerably smaller than her grandmother's Griswold house, they had many free-growing plants and a sense of open space. However, Rennie was excluded from whatever possibilities were offered when her father told her that she was just like her mother. She never returned.

Then, for the first time in the novel, another voice begins to narrate. It is Lora's voice, and she too starts talking about her background. Somewhat surprisingly, and coincidentally, Lora is also a Canadian; like Rennie, she has bad memories of cellars. However, her stories, as she had earlier assured Rennie they would be, are "tabloid" stories that, we are led to believe, emerge from her working-class roots. She vividly describes being molested by her step-father, the most unsavoury character in the novel. Hired to help out with odd jobs around the apartment complex where he lived with Lora and her mother, he spent most of his time sitting at the kitchen table in an old grey sweater. Because he limped, he could not hold down a full-time job and, because he disapproved of the government, refused pension and welfare cheques. As a result, Lora's mother had a hard time keeping the family together. At one point, to prevent her husband from losing his temper every time Lora bumped into him, she tells Lora to "pretend he's a closed door" (112). Lora describes her early life as "sleepwalking" and, in retrospect, admits that her growing years had been like standing on "the edge of this cliff" (113). Like Rennie's life now, so had Lora's life been then, filled with a fear of bodily harm and a persistent uneasiness about what might happen next.

It is Lora who initially discusses what Atwood defines as power in the essay "An End to Audience."[3] Lora says, about Bob, when Rennie questions the rationale of his violence: "He hit me because he could get away with it and nobody could stop him. That's mostly why people do stuff like that, because they can get away with it" (SW 114). This definition of power alters the novel's terms of reference for Rennie, and for the reader. As long as we remain a part of Rennie's middle-class family, by participating only in Rennie's life, the unspeakable remains unspeakable. Middle-class decorum covers underlying violence. But if we are to understand this novel, we must listen to what Lora tells us. Sexual relationships, in Lora's world, are brutal; men prey on women. As she talks about her mother, Lora admits that she now understands that her mother had probably wanted to get away as badly as Lora did herself, but that "she didn't know how to get out" (115). Instead, she hoped. She believed that "good luck was out there somewhere and it was waiting for her" (115). Just as she will learn about wanting out, so Rennie will also learn about good luck.

After Lora's story, the narrative abruptly jumps back to Rennie. She is dreaming. She has returned to her grandmother's garden which has reverted to its original shape: "everything is so bright, so full of juice, the red zinnias, the hollyhocks, the sunflowers like vivid bees around them." This heavenly vision is marred only by the fact that it is winter and "small icicles hang from the stems and blossoms" (115). When her grandmother appears clothed in a white summer dress covered with blue flowers, Rennie recognizes death. In the background, she hears her mother and her aunts singing in three-part harmony, but when she tries to touch her grandmother, her hands go through her. "Life everlasting" (115), says her grandmother.

Rennie struggles to wake up, and believes that she has. Now, she is in bed, the sheets twisted around her, in a dim room. She's "wearing a long white cotton gown" (116) which ties at the back, although she denies that she is in a hospital. She struggles up and over to her bureau, where she opens the drawers and, as if she were her grandmother, begins to search for her hands.

A third time she wakes up. And on this occasion, the passage combines images of suffocation and enclosure with those of suspension. But even when she is apparently awake, Rennie remains caught in some in-between world: "It's dawn, the noises are beginning, the mosquito netting hangs around her in the warm air like mist. She sees where she is, she's here, by herself, she's stranded in the future. She doesn't know how to get back" (116). These sentences do not tell us where "back" is, nor do they clarify Rennie's position when she is "stranded in the future." They do, however, suggest that wherever she is, she is by herself. By association, the narrative moves on to a discussion of dreams. Rennie recalls asking Jake about his dreams, and as with almost all her conversations with him, he responded with sexual suggestions. When Rennie asked Daniel the same question, he claimed he could not remember dreaming at all.

Following this "dream" section, the plot moves to the Sunset Inn, where Rennie is just getting up. On this day, she has promised to pick up Elva's heart medicine at the airport. The taxi she takes is a hearse-like vehicle, "upholstered in mauve shag" (118); the driver wears a cross around his neck. At the customs office, Rennie is surprised when she is handed a large box. After some dispute — she naturally thought the parcel would be much smaller — during which she feels that her "sense of correct procedure is being violated" (120), she drags the box, which "weighs a ton" (120), through the front door, gets back into the taxi and — the scene seems surreal — listens to "I'm Dreaming of a White Christmas" on the return trip.

Various reviewers and critics have vociferously objected to the depiction of Rennie's naïveté during these events. We need to keep their objections in mind. Indeed, the whole episode is so bizarre, so filled with innuendo and threat, that it lacks whatever qualities we have come to accept as realistic. The dream-like (nightmarish?) atmosphere continues as Rennie drags the box up the stairs to her room at the Sunset Inn, where she slides it, like a memento of death, under her bed. We are told again about the oppressive heat, and reminded of Rennie's wound. When she looks at the biscuits brought by the waitess, she sees that their centres are "dabbed with putty-like red jam" (123).

In fact, this segment sets the tone for an investigation of the island's politics. Dr. Minnow comes to the inn, ostensibly to take Rennie to the Botanic Gardens, but actually to take her to the island's Fort Industry. On the way, he warns Rennie, who tries hard not to understand, that " 'everyone is in politics here. . . . All the time' " (124), assuring her that whatever this kind of involvement means differs dramatically from that of the "sweet Canadians."

Rennie's visit to Fort Industry should function for her, and for the reader, as a dramatic warning of danger. The Fort is surrounded by a wilderness area that sharply contrasts with Rennie's earlier dream of her grandmother's garden. Rennie sees "a field of sorts, rutted partially dried mud with a little grass growing on it." When she steps out of the car, she recognizes the "smell of bodies, of latrines and lime and decaying food" (125). Dr. Minnow carefully explains that the hurricane relief money sent from the Canadian government has not helped to rebuild the houses of the poor but has gone into the pockets of government officials; as evidence, he shows her the yard of the fort filled with women and children living in tents. Faced with such poverty and distress, Rennie thinks about her status as "a tourist. A spectator, a voyeur" (125); she could well add, a Canadian. Although the beginnings of a raised consciousness foretell changes in her attitudes, here, as elsewhere, Rennie protects herself by sliding into memories of the past. When she sees one of the yard women nursing a baby, she thinks of her own desire for a child. Jake did not want to be burdened with one, and Daniel has told her that she should wait before subjecting herself to the hormonal changes of pregnancy.

Rennie also protects herself by continuing to play the part of journalist. She takes pictures of some children in the yard, even though the pretense does not comfort her. The violent heat from the noonday sun makes her tense and anxious, and even increasingly fearful. She admits to not being a brave traveller, although she considers herself a good travel writer, and is uneasily aware of being held "captive" by a man who talks of the British as if they were a "vanished tribe" and he an archeologist "exhuming their garbage dumps" (127). As Rennie looks out to sea, towards St. Antoine's twin island of Ste. Agathe, Dr. Minnow damns the colonizers: "The British make a big mistake in the nineteenth century, they put us all together in one country. Ever since then we have trouble, and now the British have got rid of us so they can have their cheap bananas without the bother of governing us, and we have more trouble" (128). Below them, they see Marsdon campaigning for the Prince of Peace, while in the fort's yard, a car containing two men whose eyes are obscured by mirror sunglassess, arrives. With some irony, Dr. Minnow claims they are protecting him.

But Minnow's real reasons for bringing Rennie to Fort Industry become clear when he takes her to a "subterranean" part of the complex which houses army barracks. As they go down, they speak to several women employed in making crafts; Rennie buys one of the crocheted objects and Minnow tells the women that Rennie is "writing about the history here" (130). This time, although she continues to believe that he has misunderstood her assignment, she does not correct him. During this scene, as with the episode with Elva's box, Rennie appears excessively naïve. Gaining certain narrative advantages through Rennie's stance, the author has, by contrast, made the horror of the political nightmares occurring on the island all the greater. The women, Rennie learns, are prisoners; she has bought crafts from one who has chopped up another woman. Scrawled on the walls, slogans with a darkly biblical ring announce "DOWN WITH BABYLON"; "LOVE TO ALL" (131). Rennie's uneasiness increases; the barracks are "too much like a cellar" (131). But Dr. Minnow particularly wants her to see the fort's courtyard. Another wilderness area, "overgrown with weeds" and filled with rooting pigs, Rennie sees in its centre what, surely from a Canadian perspective, she imagines to be a "child's playhouse" (131). Actually, it is a gallows which Minnow wants her to photograph for her "sweet Canadians."

Time jumps. Now at lunch with Rennie at a Chinese restaurant, Dr. Minnow talks to her about drug usage among the Carib Indians. He suggests that she include in her article references to the ritual drug enemas used by the Caribs for religious purposes. This information, kinky enough to get her attention, she considers using in her *Visor* article. After all, she and her readers know about drugs and pay attention to sex. Briefly, she suspects Minnow's attention to her to be sexually motivated, mostly because she finds his sincerity impossible to interpret otherwise, different as it is from the attitudes of the superficial, fast-talking people she knows best. When he describes the curse of loving one's country too much and claims, probably from his experiences in Canada, that it is much easier to live as a foreigner in someone else's country, removed from temptations to change the political system, Rennie feels embarrassed. Sensitive to her own position as a tourist, she dislikes discussing politics. Minnow, however, will not be deflected; he insists on her involvement. We discover that the island's current election is the first since the departure of the British, and that it betrays problems common in post-colonial situations. The British parliamentary system, created through a long history of trial and error, seems spectacularly unsuited to the Caribbean, for one reason because tradition, as Dr. Minnow points out, implies that certain activities become simply "inconceivable" (133). On St. Antoine, nothing is. He wants Rennie to write about this difference, to "look" with her eyes open. Since she is a reporter, he tells her, " 'it is your duty to report' " (134).

Rennie resists this "duty" and continues to feel uneasy. The word "blood" is mentioned, and it rings in sharp contrast to the pallid "tiny corncobs," the "things that looked like steamed erasers" and the "greens and squid" (134) Rennie is about to eat. Dr. Minnow presses on, supplying Rennie with facts for her article: the seventy-percent unemployment on the island, the misuse of the hurricane funds, Ellis's purchase of the island's only newspaper, and the threats designed to win him the election. Rennie refuses to respond. Outrage, she believes, is "out of date" (135), and since nothing has happened as far as she can see, an article on the elections, she tells Minnow, would hardly be of "general interest" (135). His response has become one of the most frequently quoted statements of the novel: " 'There is no longer any place that is not of general interest. . . . The sweet Canadians have not learned this yet' " (135).

As a comment on Canada's assumed neutrality, partially the result of her marginal position on a world stage where superpowers battle over territory and direction, the statement is damning. It expresses one of Atwood's own beliefs. In the essay, "Amnesty International," she points out that Canada's "record on civil rights issues is less than pristine" (sw 395), for example in dealing with native peoples, or with the Japanese citizens interned during World War Two, or with the people arrested and jailed without warrants or explanations when the War Measures Act was invoked at the beginning of the 1970s. Dr. Minnow's words are, I believe, at the very heart of *Bodily Harm*. Rennie's desire to remain invisible and uninvolved and her silence when speech is needed mark her as diseased and, by implication, reveal the immorality of Canada's pretense of a neutrality no longer possible. Refusal to take the United States seriously also proves to be a mistake. Rennie thinks, "The CIA has been done to death; surely by now it's a joke" (135). Following the Gulf War, the world also understands better the power of oil. Minnow points out that the islands of the Caribbean are in a direct line for the shipment of oil between Venezuela and Cuba, and that whoever controls them, " 'controls the transport of oil to the United States' " (136). This argument applies as well to drug shipments, and to the shipment of weapons.

Although Dr. Minnow does not immediately alter Rennie's "life-styles" mentality, even when he uses irony to insist that he *is* talking about life-styles (what people wear; what they eat), he has succeeded in further raising her consciousness. She has been goaded into buying an island newspaper. But she has difficulty concentrating on news when she remembers that she is dying, and forgives herself for giving into the immediate physical pleasures of eating and sleeping. Back at the motel, having been warned by the Englishwoman to keep away from Dr. Minnow, Rennie notices an article on the hurricane relief fund, and another about Canada's sponsorship of a diver-training program. Both articles seem to support Dr. Minnow's information. In her room, the paper's Problem Corner reminds her of her own problems and, tangled in the mosquito netting, she thinks about Daniel. Somewhere, a voice, last heard at the end of Part One, says *"Oh please"* (140).

Politics continues to perturb her. Thinking about her life in Canada, she imagines Daniel as her opposite because he does not have even the most peripheral interest in life styles, paying little attention to where he lives, what he eats, and what he wears. He has been a good Canadian, a "dutiful husband, a dutiful parent, a dutiful son" (142), while Rennie considers duty, like outrage, passé. Nonetheless, Rennie and Daniel similarly ignore politics. Religion also plays around the edges of Rennie's consciousness. She thinks of Daniel as a saviour who resurrects women. As Christianity has always taught its followers, Rennie believes that he understands that the body is "only provisional" (143), an expression that projects her into another transitional state. Suspended in the motel room where she seems to be waiting for something to happen, and in her memories, where she waits for Daniel to make some decisions, she wonders if Daniel imagines her only as an escape, a "window but not a door" (143).

This expression reminds us of Lora's mother instructing Lora to treat Bob as if he were a door. Another image resonates — Rennie holding hands with Daniel and, for hours afterwards, feeling the shape of his hand in hers.

Readers must gather all these clues — politics, religion, love — even while being moved forward by the plot. A loud knocking on the door prefaces Paul's entrance; he has come to check up on Elva's package. Rennie still refuses to focus on the meaning of the box, and makes no response to his instructions that she take it to Ste. Agathe. This silence underscores her conscious suppression of evidence. Like many of us, she wants to go on believing that invisibility and silence will exempt her from responsible involvement. But as she and Paul step out onto the street, she sees something that forces her to look: two policemen beating up the deaf and dumb man who had earlier offered her luck. Rennie notices that the policemen are wearing shoes (the old man is still barefoot) and are kicking him. Experiencing an epiphany, Rennie understands at last that what she observes is not a picture.

Her shift from voyeurism to "seeing" begins here, although she continues to avoid acting on her growing understanding. Underlining the politics of voyeurism, Paul explains that the policemen do not like to be observed. But Rennie is now completely involved. When the old man, blood streaming from his head, looks up, she understands that "she's been seen, she's being seen with utter thoroughness, she won't be forgotten" (146). The man also makes a sound, "a stifled reaching out for speech which is worse than plain silence" (147). The painful struggle towards language has begun.

At the Driftwood, a dance is in progress; cameras flash. The stiff-legged couples who are dancing strike Rennie as "the usual bunch" (148), probably Wisconsin tourists. But she has read the signs wrong. Paul tells her that they are Swedes. He also fills her in on the natives' attitude to white women who, they believe, "lower the moral tone" (149). Paul insists that the Women's Lib Movement, which the islanders believe to be an excuse for lazy white women to hire black women to do their work for them, has exacerbated the dislike. Racial and class inequalities in the Women's Movement were certainly major issues during the 1980s, and Atwood, with her usual prescience, sees such inequalities as yet another example of unfair power distribution, a political problem. Paul continues to emphasize duplicity and secrecy. He tells Rennie that " 'nobody here is who they say they are,' " and that " 'in this place you get at least three versions of everything, and if you're lucky one of them is true' " (150). Apart from stressing luck, this comment, like Atwood's poem "True Stories," suggests that "the true story is vicious / and multiple and untrue" (TS 11). As we investigate the different perspectives of *Bodily Harm*, one may be "true," but what "truth" means, or how luck may help us are far from clear.

However, no longer completely naïve, Rennie has begun to double read; she becomes less introverted as greater involvement helps her forget that part of her is "missing" (152). Rather than existing in "blank space," events begin to assume shape for her. Walking down the hall of the Sunset Inn, she recalls a film about "the effects of atomic radiation on the courtship instincts of animals" (156) and wonders if "a few too many deadly rays zapping the pineal gland" (156) have caused fundamental changes in sexual relationships. Her focus shifts to the body that has most recently captured her attention, that of the deaf and dumb man and, forebodingly, when she enters her room she knows that once again someone has invaded her space.

By this point in *Bodily Harm*, every incident and statement reverberates with multiple meanings. For example, Rennie's invaded motel room parallels her invaded Toronto apartment which parallels her cancer-invaded body. Rennie assumes the motel intruder (as in the apartment) to be a man who has effected an eerily similar break-in. Neither has taken anything, although both have entered a locked room to go through Rennie's personal possesssions. This time, however, while the Toronto policemen seemed to be victimizing Rennie when they hinted at her involvement, when she looks under the bed and finds that Elva's package has been opened, she knows that she has participated in deceit. What she has prevented herself from even imagining stares back at her: "the front end of a small machine gun" (158). Characteristically, she immediately tries to suppress her knowledge by closing the flap, pushing "the box as far under the bed as it will go," and rearranging "the chenille coverlet" (158–59). This image splendidly illustrates repression and denial. Nonetheless, Rennie understands the threat of her involvement, tacky as that may be, and sets up her mental Clue board, converting the "faceless stranger" into "Mr. X, in the bedroom, with a knife" (159). Part Three, like the two earlier parts, ends with Rennie in the motel room, lying on the bed in the dark, alone: "She wants somebody to be with her, she wants somebody to be with. A warm body, she doesn't much care whose" (159).

As in the two earlier sections, the images of Part Three are graphic. References to broken bodies proliferate as the novel pounds home its title's multiple meanings. Lora describes being beaten up; Rennie mentions her first period and obsesses about detached hands. She remembers Jake "squeezing her breast harder" (117), and thinks about Elva's bad heart. At Fort Industry, she has met a woman who chopped up another woman; a little later, she finds troubling the fleshy body of the Englishwoman who runs the motel. Sitting in the lounge, Rennie watches her climb a ladder to take down some Christmas decorations, sees her "solid white-marbled calves" and inhales the "smell of women's washrooms: tepid flesh, face powder, ammonia" (138–39). She thinks about all the women who have had a "bite taken out of them" (142). The "bodily harm" to which the deaf and dumb man has been subjected changes Rennie from being a voyeur, to becoming the object of the old man's gaze. His suffering becomes hers. Bodies assume political meaning.

As a result, language, too, becomes more problematic. Rennie questions words like "home." Used by her father when he came for his Christmas visit, the word rang false even then. The *unheimlich* marks this novel, and although Rennie thinks that she wants to be at home, whether she means by this word her grandmother's house about which she dreams, her empty apartment in Toronto or, more generally, Canada itself, remains unclear. She wants to be at home in her body, but cancer has made that body *unheimlich*. The words "nice" and "sweet" are used ironically, and communication frequently breaks down. When Rennie tries to explain to some children that she does not have a Polaroid camera, she finds it "hard to make them understand" (127). She carries the word "duty" with her from Griswold, where it has one meaning, into her conversation with Dr. Minnow, where it has others.

Colours are also important, particularly red. Rennie dreams of her grandmother's garden, with its "red zinnias" and "scarlet runner beans" (115), eats biscuits "dabbed with putty-like red jam" (123), and drives with Dr. Minnow in a "maroon Fiat" (124). The face of the deaf and dumb man streams with red blood as the policemen beat him. Tourists burn bright pink in the local sun, while tropical hibiscus flowers flame a brilliant red. The colour white also recurs. The section opens with references to Christmas in Canada, and these are picked up again as the taxi's radio plays "I'm Dreaming of a White Christmas." When Rennie dreams of her grandmother, she sees her in a "white cotton dress with small blue flowers on it" (115), and dreams of herself in a "long white cotton gown" (116). She buys a white, crocheted object at Fort Industry, and eats white biscuits at the Sunset Inn. Like most of the other tourists, Rennie has white skin, a whiteness exaggerated in the Englishwoman who, Rennie notices, comes into the lounge "white-faced, tight-lipped" (138). Apart from suggesting blood with the repeated use of the colour red, *Bodily Harm* also emphasizes skin colours in a country where white colonialism has left many residues, and where white tourists contrast sharply with black natives. These contrasting colours draw our attention to the act of reading, for the page is white, the print black. Common to postmodern commentary, such a reference is not far-fetched; this novel parallels bodies and pages. Daniel has told Rennie to think of herself as a clean page and Rennie imagines Jake doodling on her as if she were a blank piece of paper. Colours are attached to the names of characters in the game of Clue, while national flags, through their colours, evoke patriotism.

In Part Three, then, Rennie has begun to experience a different kind of dis/ease. She is becoming conscious of her involvement in events she does not understand; "she feels that she has been either duped or used, but she isn't sure which or how" (120). She recognizes that, on St. Antoine, she is not "at home"; she has the wrong colour of skin, and stays at the wrong motel. She sees the gardens of the past turning into the wastelands of the present. Like T.S. Eliot's Prufrock, she tries to get her strength from "tea and biscuits" (122),[4] but the tea is weak, the biscuits stale. Her body continues to decay.

PART FOUR (OPENING)

Unlike the first three parts, this section begins in the third person and the past tense. The narrator describes Rennie immediately after she had come out of the hospital and was looking for "support." She wanted to feel "normal" (163) again. Both words echo the language used in a hospital. She met her friend Jocasta for lunch at a Toronto restaurant and there, while drinking red wine and eating bread and spinach salad, Jocasta talked, a little too fast, about relationships between women and men. After recounting a bizarre incident she had recently experienced with a man, she summed up their difficulty as a "semantic problem," a "problem in communications, or maybe it's linguistics" (166). References to imprecise language and to linguistic confusion continue in this section. Like all the other breakdowns described, a loss of meaning, whether it be personal, political, moral or spiritual, has resulted in the invisibility, silence, and dis/ease that mark Rennie's world. When Jocasta shifted to describing the man's identity crisis, she unwittingly drew attention to the physical and emotional anguish Rennie undergoes in her struggle to maintain an identity. Jocasta also defined what she believed to be the roots of bodily harm in sexual relationships. Speaking of men, she argued that "they don't want love and understanding and meaningful relationships, they still want sex, but only if they can *take* it" (167).

Rennie's conviction that Jocasta thought her on the "brink of death" (167) ominously resonates, as do the reference to the lunch as "a cheerful bedside visit in the terminal ward" (168) and the expression "out-of-control cell division" (168). As we have seen throughout earlier sections, Rennie's obsession with her diseased body colors her view of the world. Part Four transmits a growing sense of impending doom. After the lunch with Jocasta, Rennie returned to the apartment and found Jake, sitting in a chair in the middle of the day, his eyes puffy. She realized that the two of them were in the process of "competing for each other's pity" (168). Jake's words, "we should try again" (168) also ambiguously echo hospital conversation.

Then the narrative breaks, and we return to the storyteller, Lora. In her second narration, she continues with the story of her past from the point where she stopped in Part Three. She has arrived at the age of sixteen, at adolescent sexuality, and again, she begins with bodily harm. She talks about a schoolgirl who attempted abortion with a knitting needle. On the other hand, she describes her own virginity as a class issue; the "nice," or to use Rennie's family's word, the "decent" girls, according to Lora, were the ones who got into trouble. Lora's working-class boyfriend did not think he was the "cat's ass" (169), as the rich boys did. Such boys did not ask girls like Lora out on dates, although they were more than willing to have sex with them. Lora was smart enough to stay away from them. But, like everyone else in this novel, Lora cannot avoid bodily harm. When she and her boyfriend decided to get married, she let him "go all the way" (170), and when she returned to her apartment, her stepfather, aroused, grabbed her breast. She recalls his "grey teeth," and the "black gums around the edges" (171). In defense, she attacked Bob with the prong of a can opener, and he fell onto some broken lightbulbs.

This section stresses transgressed boundaries, for example between poor and rich, and between fathers and daughters. It also focuses on bodies, particularly breasts, and on opened flesh. Sharp objects, knitting needles, can openers, broken glass, cause physical harm. After the attack, Lora left home. She tells Rennie that her mother blamed her for what had happened with Bob. These events thus also psychologically reflect some of what we know about Rennie, who insists that her mother would blame her even for contracting cancer. Coincidences between Lora's and Rennie's lives are, I suggest, clues to help us read the novel's board game.

At this point, the novel moves into another of the suspensions that Rennie experiences with uncanny regularity. This time, we are told, Rennie is having a harder and harder time crossing the line between waking and sleeping. Now she seems to be in a space somewhere between life and death. The scenario, clearly drawn, shows us an operating room, with Rennie in the process of being opened up. She feels divided into two parts, one of which floats up around the ceiling, where the air-conditioning unit emits a steady hum, the other of which lies on a table, covered with a "green cloth." Around this body, faceless strangers hidden behind masks are in the "middle of a performance, a procedure, an incision" (172). But instead of a description of a cancerous breast, Rennie sees her heart, like the dot on the digital clock of her radio alarm at the Sunset Inn, "squeezing away, a fist opening and closing around a ball of blood." It is "the heart they're after" (172–73). This striking image brings to a critical point impressions that have been building throughout: a noise overhead; a pulsing, rhythmic beating; a divided consciousness; the cutting open of flesh. A few sentences later, the mosquito netting around Rennie's bed at the Sunset Inn, like the ether mask used during an operation, covers her face, merging with the line between sleeping and waking that Rennie has increasing difficulty crossing.

Is this passage taking place in whatever passes for the novel's present, as the verb tense would suggest? Are we meant to configure the novel's Clue board as the doctor in the hospital with the knife? The emphasis on the heart certainly suggests an emotional opening that deepens the effects of Rennie's partial mastectomy. This operation exposes her to new ways of seeing.

Apparently still at the Sunset Inn, Rennie continues to suffer tension as the box under the bed emits waves of malevolence. She admits that she does not want to leave it in her room while she goes for breakfast for fear "it will hatch and something unpleasant will emerge" (173). Her decision to tape the box shut so that it will appear unopened reflects her awareness of a body that she wants to keep shut; she struggles with her fear of death. Then, leaving her passport in the motel's safe (a loss of identity she will later regret), she sets off with the box in tow, to board the boat to Ste. Agathe. She hires a boy with a wheelbarrow to take the box to the harbour, following him as he runs through a labyrinth of back streets, past mounds of rotting fruit and vegetables. Unable to interpret the boy's smile, or the shouted comments he has made on the way, Rennie is further bewildered and frightened by the shoving crowd of boys who try to put her things on the boat. Moreover, she is overwhelmed with guilt. She connects this sensation to an episode with Jake when the two of them had been stopped for speeding, while the marijuana she knew was in the glove compartment made her feel guilt "shining around her like a halo" (175). Now, to divert attention from herself, she falls back into the pretense of journalism, looking for subjects to photograph. The boat in front of her is called *Memory*, and Rennie takes a picture of the men loading her.

When Lora suddenly joins her, Rennie is torn between anger (she's been duped), and fear. She rejects the idea of asking more questions, suspecting that "one question too many may take her somewhere she definitely doesn't want to go" (176). Lora warns her not to sit in the boat's cabin, where you " 'just about choke to death' " (177); like many other enclosed places in the novel, the cabin threatens to suffocate its occupants. In yet another of *Bodily Harm*'s bizarre coincidences, people whom Rennie has seen elsewhere join her on the boat: the bird-watching couple; the German women. As Rennie observes the boat pulling away from the shore, she imagines the widening space as a "split, a gap" (178). The maroon car that draws up to the harbour as the boat leaves is the one Rennie saw at Fort

Industry; the faceless men in mirror sunglasses get out to watch the departure. So it is that every image, description, and incident imply threat. As the boat nears Ste. Agathe, Rennie sees the island as a dry "line of harsh vertical cliffs flat-topped and scrubby," while the retreating St. Antoine, from this perspective, looks "moist green" (178), like a postcard, even though Rennie also recognizes the outlines of Fort Industry. The boat's sails bell out in the wind, reminding Rennie of her mother's clean sheets, and the expression "dirty laundry" floats into her mind. She feels queasy. The bottom of the boat is littered with drinking men.

On the boat, Lora and Rennie talk about the CIA as Atwood, in an interview, claimed people in the West Indies frequently do, discussing who is spying on whom. Lora names the apparently harmless and elderly bird-watching couple as the current agents, and although surprised, Rennie knows that her own information, limited and incomplete, will not enlighten her. Surfaces deceive. When the boat arrives at Ste. Agathe's harbour, people swarm to the dock to pick up bread and eggs, and the people on the boat crowd to get off. Elva waits for her box (no one pretends any longer that it contains heart medicine) and when she gets it, carries it off on her head. As usual, Rennie misses the meaning of events, and mistakes their tone. When Lora comments that " 'this place is crawling with grandmothers' " (184), and begins discussing the colonial mind-set of the island people, readers should recognize her irony, even though Rennie does not.

Rennie continues to misread signs. Although the island is crowded because of the election, she is surprised at the scarcity of accommodation. She also remains naïve about politics. When Lora tells her that Ellis controls the island and does not appreciate the threat posed by Dr. Minnow, Rennie, still thinking as a Canadian, asks: " 'If this man is so terrible . . . why does he keep getting elected?' " (185). Many readers, whether "sweet Canadians" or not, share Rennie's unquestioned assumption that democracy functions effectively everywhere, a misreading, Atwood implies, that results from a tourist mentality that may well lead to bodily harm. Rennie decides that a couple she sees are tourists, that "they're people like her, transients; like her they can look all they want to, they're under no obligation to see, they can take pictures of anything they wish" (185). But her judgement cannot be trusted. As she sits drinking at the Lime Tree, she straddles radically different worlds. When the bird-watching couple joins her, in spite of Lora's information, Rennie assumes her Canadian manners, talking to the man and woman politely and deciding "that Lora must be wrong." The "innocuous," the "kindly," and the "boring" (187) do not jibe with her concept of spies.

She has been drinking steadily and her consequent fuzziness also makes her point of view suspect. As she leaves the Lime Tree, she runs into Dr. Minnow who introduces her to the man she had seen on the plane, "the white man in the safari jacket" (28), who turns out to be a fellow Canadian. Rennie assures him that she writes only on subjects like food, emphasizing, for Dr. Minnow's benefit, her continued rejection of his request that she write about what she sees happening around her. Minnow continues to give her facts, this time about the forthcoming election, and as the two men move toward the bar, we are told that the "neutral-coloured Canadian" (191) follows Minnow.

A more disruptive incident occurs as well. One of the German women — earlier, the elderly couple had spoken of contemporary German wealth — has injured her foot by stepping on a sea urchin. The injury is significant enough to remind us of the cover of the original hardback copy of the Canadian edition of the novel. On it, according to Atwood, is a "scientific drawing from the 19th century of a marine organism,"⁵ spines radiating, promising bodily harm. The accident brings Elva back into the action, this time as a healer. Although the German woman has been "invaded" (192), the poison working itself through her system, Elva claims that she can cure her. She says: " 'It's in the hands. . . . It's a gift, I have it from my grandmother' " (193). Both allusive and elusive, the recurring motifs of hands, grandmothers, and gifts seem uncanny and the suggestions of healing remind us that Rennie, as any cancer patient does, contemplates miracle cures. As she watches Elva work, she longs to "put herself into the care of those magic hands" (194).

Joined by Paul, Rennie walks back with him through yet another garden, this one "full of trees, flowering, overgrown, limes and lemons and something else, odd reddish-orange husks split open to show a white core and three huge black seeds like the eyes of insects" (194). This evocative passage reminds us of Rennie's breast which, like the "reddish-orange husks," has been split open to expose the

64

underlying disease. The garden also triggers Rennie's memories of Daniel, and her desire to be "touched by him" (195), to open him up, to close the "gap between what she wanted and where she was" (196). But the fissure remains. Daniel cannot save her, even though he, like Elva, has his soul in his hands. Rennie knows that if they were cut off, "he'd be a zombie" (198). She also thinks of Jake. Following her surgery, she had not wanted him to touch her and the painful efforts made by both of them to overcome what Rennie describes as her dislike of being seen "the way she was, damaged, amputated" (198), seemed funereal. She remembers being arranged on the bed, dressed in black, with candles around her and although she tried to pretend that everything was normal, she felt as if "the words in her head came one at a time, as if they were being spoken by someone else" (200). Again, this statement points to the words of *Bodily Harm* itself, where Rennie's words often seem to be spoken by someone else. Also, because she seemed more open, more vulnerable, Jake did not have to fight her for sex; as Jocasta suggested, about men in general, "they still want sex, but only if they can *take* it" (167). The ambiguous phrase "*oh please*" (201) reappears, apparently out of nowhere.

Paul and Rennie head toward Paul's house, where Rennie has agreed to stay, the hotels, as Lora had predicted, being full. They pass some young girls, singing a hymn in three-part harmony, just as Rennie's mother had sung three-part harmony with Rennie's aunts in Griswold. As if to emphasize the connection, Rennie sees the girls' clothing as oddly old-fashioned. The garden outside Paul's house is filled with rocks and cacti, and some dying shrubs with a "many-stranded yellow vine covering them like a net" (202). Inside, objects like a telescope and a navigational map on an otherwise empty wall arouse our suspicion. Drinking once again, Rennie watches the sunset (we think of the Sunset Inn) and, as if she were in a motel room, or a hospital, finds the bed "expertly made, hospital corners firmly tucked in " (203). It too has a mosquito net around it. Dressed completely in white, Rennie prepares to sleep with Paul. Unlike her final coupling with Jake, when she asked for dope, this time she already feels "insubstantial, as if she's died and gone to heaven and come back minus a body" (203). This suspended state dramatizes the narrative's split perspective (the interaction between objectivity and subjectivity) and reflects the tourist mentality described and questioned throughout. Indeed, Rennie believes that suspension means that "there's nothing to worry about, nothing can touch her. She's a tourist. She's exempt" (203). By believing in exemption, as Paul has earlier encouraged her to do, she effectively distances herself from serious problems and avoids commiting herself to any particular course of action.

The last paragraph of Part Four comes to a close, for the first time in the novel, with Rennie with someone else. Although she lies in a bedroom as usual, Paul has joined her and this time, instead of experiencing smothering enclosure, she is "opened" (204). For a brief moment, she feels whole. The paragraph is nonetheless unsettling. Touching matters here, as it does in many other places, but the language used implies that Rennie may be close to death. She imagines the sexual act as "only the body's desperation, a flareup, a last clutch at the world before the long slide into a final illness and death" (204), and expressions like "she's still here on the earth" and "she can still be touched" (204) seem more appropriate to someone imagining torture, or undergoing an operation, than to someone making love.

Many themes and images in this section suggest opening and closing. Jocasta began her conversation with Rennie by calling herself an "open book" (164). While doctors cut into Rennie on the operating table, her heart is "opening and closing" (173). She tapes closed the gun box, which has been opened by an anonymous invader who has broken open the locked door of Rennie's room. The sea urchin cuts open the German woman's foot, and while Elva works on her, the woman opens and closes her eyes. Rennie talks about how she has wanted to open Daniel up. The section leads to Rennie's intercourse with Paul during which, we are told, Rennie is "open now, she's been opened" (204).

References to bright colours continue to vitalize other, more drab, language. Red wine and blue silk roses dominated the table where Rennie and Jocasta had lunch, and Jocasta mentioned wearing a "fabulous black knitted sheath" (165). The United Appeals thermometer, referred to in one of Jocasta's similes, marks campaign donations with a red line, while Rennie undergoes her operation covered by a green cloth, one mark of colour in the pristine whiteness of the room. In the distance, Ste. Agathe seems to be a blue shape. Lora shows up in "cerise" with "blue orchids" (176) and Elva appears in "a pink cotton skirt with red flamingoes on it" (183). Contrasts between black and white skin — and the boiled pink of the white sunbathers — emphasize race; for example, Elva does not speak to Lora, who is white, because she lives with Elva's son, Prince, a black man. The hotels scattered on Ste. Agathe's hillside are predominantly white, a young girl at the Lime Tree wears a "white dress" (185), and the candles being lit for dinner are in "little red glass chimneys" (189), suggestive of the votive candles in churches. "Reddish-orange husks" ripen and burst in the Lime Tree's garden. Rennie recalls Jake, wrapped in a blue towel, coming into the bedroom where she lay in black underwear: black and blue. At Paul's, Rennie wears "a white shirt and a wrap skirt, also white" (203). In fact, she almost always dresses in white.

As she has from the beginning, Rennie drifts in and out of various drugged states. Therefore, she needs support, and expressions like "support systems" and "support groups" draw attention to Rennie's efforts to maintain her "balance" (168). When she went to meet Jocasta at the restaurant, we are told that she "made it to the restaurant in the usual way, one foot in front of the other on a sidewalk that wasn't really there," knowing that "it was important to keep your balance" (163). At the Lime Tree, Rennie drinks rum and lime, and feels the rum "going right into her, smoothing her down from the inside" (185). After her third drink, she becomes "fuzzy" (188). She recalls that she and Jake used to smoke dope when they made love, effectively distancing themselves from their bodies.

Gaps occur, not only as part of the narrative's content, but also in its temporal discontinuities and spatial orientations. Readers, like the characters of the novel, seem to be missing crucial bits of information. The boys waiting around the harbour "draw back into a circle, leaving a gap" for Rennie to enter (175). Later, as the boat casts off, Rennie watches the water growing between her and the boat, seeing the space as a "split, a gap" (178). Breaks in the text, marked by white spaces, emphasize discontinuity, and implied distances between observation and interpretation persistently unsettle readers. Rennie feels split into two parts, her body and mind separated, her observing eye cut off from her sensual experience. About Daniel, she confesses that "there was such a gap between what she wanted and where she was that she could hardly stand it" (196), and imagines telling Paul before they make love, "There's part of me missing" (203). This emphasis on holes becomes even more insistent in Part Five.

PART FIVE (HOLES)

Part Five begins curtly with a description of Rennie's sado-masochistic relationship with Jake. We are told that Jake had enjoyed hurting Rennie, even as he persuaded her that his desire to win at sexual competition was a game. Apparently, the word "game" makes sadistic behaviour acceptable; by extension, if Rennie were afraid, she would be guilty of poor sportsmanship.

Yet what follows the opening paragraph does not seem like pretense. *Visor's* managing editor decided that it would be "sort of fun" for Rennie to write an article on pornography in order to balance the "heavy and humourless" (207) anti-pornography pieces appearing in feminist journals and the feminist press. We think of the work of feminist scholars published around the same time as *Bodily Harm*, Susan Griffin's *Pornography and Silence*, Andrea Dworkin's *Pornography: Men Possessing Women and Women Hating*, and Catherine MacKinnon's *Sexual Harassment of Working Women*. *Bodily Harm* emphasizes the evils of pornography by connecting them with games and playfulness. In Atwood's earlier short story, "Rape Fantasies," four women, treated ironically, describe their sexual fantasies; one woman believes that if a woman talks to her attacker, she should be able to prevent him from going "ahead with it" (DG 110). The later novel pushes irony further. Doing research for the proposed *Visor* article, Rennie visited a male artist who specialized in sculptures made from "life-sized mannequins." He turned these mannequins, "dressed in half-cup bras and G-string panties," into such objects as tables and chairs; he referred to them as "visual pun[s]" (208). They emphasize again Berger's argument that women are conventionally shown as inviting manipulation and use. The sculpture of the man, on the other hand, stood alone, dressed in a "classic blue pinstripe business suit," apparel that implies power and control, as do the "plastic dildoes" (208) glued to his head. When the artist told Rennie that art "takes what society deals out and makes it visible" (208), the reader should not miss the probable allusion to Atwood's visual politics in the carefully crafted and sensuous images of *Bodily Harm* for, somewhat like the sculptor, the author uses a female body to help her readers experience exactly what society "deals out." The novel's "themes" and "variations" (208) are composed around fundamental inequalities in gender roles.

References to "raw material" remind us also that before shaping a novel, writers must collect material (see, for example, the "Raw Materials" section of *Murder in the Dark*), just as *Bodily Harm*'s sculptor does. His raw material came from the Metro Police's Project P., an exhibit of pornography open to the public and visited by Rennie, also collecting raw material for her article, and Jocasta. A "young, fresh-faced, still eager" (209) policeman showed the collection, housed in ordinary rooms in the main police building, to the two women. At the beginning, Rennie used her job to turn her observations into language, questioning the spellling of certain objects. But Jocasta, more astutely, recognized parallels between the displayed objects and medical instruments. One bizarre item had defeated the policemen's private bets on its use, another example of connections between pornography and games. Rennie remained emotionally detached, even when the policeman took the two women into a video room to show them films of women copulating with various animals, as well as some "sex-and-death pieces," in which women were "being strangled or bludgeoned or having their nipples cut off by men dressed up as Nazis" (210). Rennie convinced herself that the pictures were not real, the blood only ketchup.

Nonetheless, despite herself, she became involved. When the policeman showed the women the "grand finale" (210), a black woman's pelvis with the "usual swollen pinkish purple" wound showing, but with the head of a rat emerging from it, Rennie "felt that a large gap had appeared in what she's been used to thinking of as reality" (210). She vomited on the policeman's shoes. Although this incident occurred one month before her mastectomy, it indicates that Rennie had already begun to be opened up. Returning to her office, she told the editor that she would not write the article, using the excuse that "there were some things it was better not to know any more about than you had to" (211). But Rennie had seen more than enough to affect her vision permanently. Even in the West Indies, where she persistently struggles to see only surfaces, she can still be pierced by memories of the pornography exhibit. Furthermore, her relationship with Jake had been affected by what she had seen. Even before her operation, she experienced difficulties in acting out her role in Jake's sexual fantasies and saw that playing the part of a passive victim so that Jake could practice his power was hardly a game. We are told that she "now felt that in some way that had never been spelled out between them he thought of her as the enemy" (211). Like the objects in the pornography exhibit, Rennie imagined herself being used as "raw material" (212).

Then, for the third time, Lora resumes her narration. As usual, she speaks in the first person, and in the present tense. Now, she discusses Paul, connecting him by narrative proximity with Rennie's Jake. She met Paul on a visit to the island after she had broken up with a husband whose sexual advances she describes as "something you let men do to you" (212). To Lora, whose life has been marked by violence, Paul seemed an unusual man; he was not "mean" (213). To be with him, she stayed in the West Indies, working on one of his boats. Now, however, Lora admits that "there was something missing in him " (214); we are becoming accustomed to hearing about missing parts. The locals claim that Paul *"does deal"* (214), meaning that he deals with the devil, because he is a loner who genuinely enjoys danger. As evidence of this proclivity, Lora recounts a story that clarifies Marsdon's hatred of Paul. When Marsdon had punished his woman's unfaithfulness by covering her naked body with cow-itch and tying her to a tree near an ant-hill, only Paul had enough nerve to free her; Lora believes this action did not result from kindness, but rather from bravado. In fact, Paul's recklessness drives Lora away; she was convinced that he endangered everyone around him.

Apart from being about male violence and thrill-seeking, Lora's stories are also about drugs; they are meant to inform Rennie. According to Lora, United States agents make sure that the boats from Colombia do not dump their drugs directly in the United States. As a result, dealers use the islands to parcel out the drugs to be carried on yachts and private planes. The Cubans, the mob, and the CIA share this lucrative business, the latter of whom lobbies Washington to keep drugs illegal and therefore valuable. As a CIA representative, Ellis cooperates with the dealers, although he attacks small drug operations to keep the competition down. By striking out on his own, Paul has made himself a target for the Cubans, the mafia and, through Ellis, the CIA. Because she likes "[her] skin the way it is, only the holes God gave me" (216), Lora has left Paul and moved in with a young, native man, Prince, a member of the local Communist party. She admits that she loves Prince because "he really believed he could save the world" (216).

A break, and we are back with Rennie who lies in bed with an apparently "tangible" (217) Paul. Hovering again between waking and sleeping, she hears a "bleating" sound that turns out to be from a goat outside the bedroom window and recognizes hymn melodies emerging from a transistor radio belonging to two men "hacking at the shrubs with machetes" (217). Perhaps dreaming, Rennie imagines that "there was another man in bed with them; something white, a stocking or a gauze bandage, wrapped around his head" (217). Like earlier ambiguous images, this faceless dream man seems oddly situated at this point in the novel, and increases our sense of the instability of the boundaries between dreams and actual life.

The third time that Rennie wakes up in this series of paragraphs, Paul has disappeared. She wanders through a house that seems so empty "it could be a motel" (217), and goes outside. In the morning light, Paul's garden appears pleasant enough: "There's a tree beside the porch, covered with pink flowers, a swarm of hummingbirds around it" (218). But as she continues to look at the garden and below it, at the road, "the whole vista" becomes "one-dimensional," a "scrim," a cover for something subterranean, possibly "the real truth" (218). This evidence of Rennie's developing consciousness (and conscience) offers further clues for our reading of the novel. If we remove the "scrim," perhaps the meaning of the novel will become clear. If we locate the peripheral sounds, such as the "desolate monotonous wail" (218) that Rennie hears coming from the east, we may discover the narrative space.

Continually emphasizing ways of seeing, the narrator tells us that when Rennie looks through Paul's telescope, immediately focussing on a woman, the telescope's intense power reveals "even the striations on her belly" (218). Again, female bodies become the center of attention. But Rennie, more conscious now of voyeurism's intrusive power, experiences embarrassment at watching someone who is unaware of her gaze and turns away. Wandering through Paul's house, she feels isolated; even the refrigerator is almost empty. The woman and two little girls in a picture in Paul's drawer look like ghosts, their eyes shadowed by the sun. Paul, too, seems like a ghost. He has left no footprints to mark his early departure and Rennie's uneasiness increases when she finds a ghost-like picture of him. She continues to look through his things, but she seems less and less like her former uncommitted, invisible self. Now, she looks actively for clues because she "wants to know"; specifically, she wants to find information that will make Paul "real" (219) for her. This language recalls a younger Rennie, at a time before she became sophisticated, back when "she believed there was a right man, not several and not almost right, and she believed there was a real story, not several and not almost real" (64).

After investigating the rather anonymous objects in Paul's bathroom, Rennie, behaving like Bluebeard's wife, a figure of interest to Atwood who called her second collection of short stories *Bluebeard's Egg*, opens another door. In the exposed room, information shouts out although Rennie retreats from enlightenment. In spite of seeing a complicated-looking radio, she "can't identify" (219) other equipment and suffers a startling amnesia about a large, familiar-looking box. When she hears someone enter the house, she leaves this "forbidden room" (220) and, suffering guilt, hides in the hallway. The intruder, however, is only Lora, and she has brought food. As they sit drinking coffee together, Rennie watches Lora's hands, "the squat fingers, the rough gnawed skin around the nails" (220). When Paul returns, Lora questions where he got eggs; he answers that he's "got connections" (221), reminding us of Lora's earlier statement that Paul is "the connection" (182).

Lora disappears and Paul and Rennie make love. Although Rennie's "thighs are aching," and she believes Paul and herself to be "transients" (222), she feels gratitude for being touched, as she did the night before. Articulating a choice offered to many cancer patients, between something and nothing, Rennie chooses something. As she and Paul shower together, she touches Paul's body and, still searching for clues, tries to find "something, his presence in his own body, the other body beneath the tangible one" (222). When the two of them step out into the "white light" (222), she ambiguously imagines the future to be a long way from the present. In his role as tour guide — he seems a most unlikely Virgil, Dante's guide through the Inferno — Paul tells Rennie that the islanders dislike tourists because their presence elevates the price of basic foods like sugar. Falling back into her superficial, life-styles lingo, Rennie suggests that no one should eat sugar, but Paul ominously corrects her by stating the obvious, that refusing sugar " 'depends on what else you have to eat' " (223). On the beach, a parade is in progress; Elva leads it, followed by Marsdon who wears boots. They march, accompanied by wooden flutes and a drum, Elva holding a white pottie and a roll of toilet paper, objects that symbolize their attitude to the opposition's election campaign.

Like returning ghosts, the two men in "mirror sunglasses" (224) appear, but this time, they are accompanied by a third man, dressed in black "like an undertaker," who turns out to be the current Minister of Justice. Rennie hears "a persistent hum" and, as she and Paul walk north, it "becomes a throb, a steady heartbeat" (224). Once again, we seem trapped inside some vaguely defined body. Paul discusses a captured thief with a woman running a store, and outside, emphasizes the man's luck. Luck has become a leitmotif in *Bodily Harm*, and although the word seems inappropriate here, Paul explains that another thief recently caught had been pounded to death, "no questions asked" (225). He also tells Rennie that the villagers sometimes chop women up, although they more often "beat or slice" (226), and when Rennie, horrified by references to dismemberment, to bodily harm, objects, Paul explains that the natives, unlike the Americans for example, have no guns.

Back at the Lime Tree, feeling "peripheral" (226), Rennie thinks about Paul's words of the night before: "Don't expect too much" (226). These echo her earlier decision that "she no longer expected Daniel. Maybe that was the right way to do it, never to expect anything" (197). But in spite of his caveat, Rennie admits that she has expected something from Paul ("something is better than nothing") and that now, these expectations seem "vast, sentimental, grandiose, technicolour, magical, ridiculous" (227), like the plot of a cheap romance. Rennie wants to "take [her] body and run" (227) from the islands. Instead, Dr. Minnow joins her, as if he were her conscience; he wants to give her more information for her article. Because she remains convinced that she will not write it, Dr. Minnow makes Rennie feel "fraudulent" (227).

He explains that Ellis may win the election because he uses dishonest tactics. For example, he has confiscated the hurricane relief money to bribe the voters of St. Antoine, although on Ste. Agathe, people think it a good joke to take Ellis's money and to vote for Dr. Minnow. Looking at his "thin hands" (228), placed tensely on the table, Rennie realizes that the man is "enraged," and that he has to hold his hands "to keep them from moving, lifting, striking out" (228). Now Ellis has altered the voting lists, replacing the names of Minnow's supporters with those of dead people so that, as Minnow says, the " 'government is being elected by corpses' " (228). Throughout this section, funereal imagery augurs ill. When Rennie questions Minnow's reasons for continuing to play out what seems to be a farce, he admits that his actions are "illogical and futile" (229), but insists that he has a "duty to imagine" (229). Like Atwood ("An End to Audience"), Minnow understands that to avoid total political repression, the imagination must be kept alive.

Screaming interrupts the discussion and Elva appears, harmed, her face "streaked, mapped, caked, dark red" (229). The scene arranges itself into a picture: a white basin, red blood, a blue washcloth, with Lora washing Elva's face. Rennie finds out that Elva has tried to strangle Ellis's undertaker-like Minister of Justice who, along with two policemen, had been beating her son, Prince. Once again, the election has caused trouble; Marsdon had started the ruckus by shouting names at the current Justice Minister who holds the position he wants himself. As Elva walks off, Rennie, who has been trying to stay uninvolved, wonders if someone should accompany her, but is assured by Lora that Elva manages quite well on her own. Lora repeats that the " 'whole place runs on grandmothers' " (231), and the word "normal" (231) hangs in the air, another of the reiterated words in this novel.

Rennie, on the road, returns to Paul's house. The heat oppresses her, and she experiences the uncanny sensation of being watched. On the hill, some schoolgirls surround her; two of them hold her hands, one on each side. They accompany her to Paul's place and, as she goes to the door, she hears them "giggling" (232) behind her. Paul's door is open (she has no key) and Rennie goes to the hammock where she lies, "waiting for time to pass" (232). What she waits for remains unclear. She watches the housekeeper's activities and although she thinks that "she ought to pretend to be doing something important" (233), remains suspended in the hammock feeling "uneasy," "superfluous," "invisible," "exposed" (233). When the woman leaves, Rennie makes a drink and lies down on the bed, the mosquito net over her. Suddenly, she feels herself being touched, perhaps by Paul, perhaps by "a faceless stranger" (233). As usual, this interruption seems unfocused and spaceless, repetitive, uncanny.

The passage that follows also appears peculiarly situated. Rennie lies in bed with Paul. Outside she hears the window rattling in the wind and, more unsettling, "a sound like the dragging of thick cloth across a floor" (233). The word "terminal," repeated from elsewhere, reminds the reader of the airport, of the bus, of Rennie's condition. Paul's empty house feels like a train station and Paul warns Rennie to leave Ste. Agathe, to get on a plane to Canada. When he suggests that she might be "too involved," Rennie thinks he refers to their affair but, almost immediately, the expression *"massive involvement"* (234), resonating like the word "terminal" with layers of meaning from its various appearances in the text, pulls the reader back to Rennie's body, even though Paul means political insurrection, and wants to get Rennie off the island so that he can remember " 'something good I've done' " (234). As Rennie imagines returning to Canada, she moves into the future tense used at the novel's conclusion. She sees herself waiting in the "steamy airport" in the Barbados, boarding the "monotonous jet," arriving at the "sterile and rectilinear" Toronto airport, and stepping out into the dull, Canadian winter, where the people, similar to those who populate T.S. Eliot's *Waste Land,* "hunched into their winter coats," scuttle "heads-down along the sidewalks" (234).[6] She decides that she has nothing to anticipate.

This realization provokes a backward look at the termination of her relationship with Jake. When he returned to the apartment to pick up some clothes and, of course, his pictures, he mentioned his "new lady" (235); for Rennie, this woman was "just a headless body, with or without a black nightgown," "a future, a space, a blank" (235). Apart from implying Rennie's refusal to imagine a "story" about Jake's new lover, these observations also emphasize contrasts marked by gender, between activity and passivity, between movement and stasis. Rennie describes "the urgency and blindness" of the male act of love, which functions quite differently from the way in which women have "darkness" thrown into them; she recalls sitting in a "well-lit visible frozen pose at the kitchen table" (236). This hospital-like frieze — the opening up; the internal darkness; the lighting; the paralyzed body — again reminds us of the game of Clue, and we are led back to the man with the rope. Jake had insisted that he himself knew the difference between "a game and the real thing," and Rennie pictured the two of them as "dead bodies." As she has noticed Dr. Minnow do, she remembers pressing her hands together "to keep them still" (236) and, further back, sees her grandmother's hands, held together in prayer.

She remembers, too, not wanting to get out of bed the day after

Jake had taken his possessions away. She thought about her doctor and, finally, phoned him at his office, implying to his nurse that she wanted to commit suicide so that the woman would believe the call to be an emergency. But when Daniel arrived, Rennie understood that he really felt physical "need," not emotional "desire," a difference that Rennie must contemplate, particularly in the Caribbean. When at last they made love, Rennie saw that Daniel was the "needy one"; she could not keep neediness to herself. The experience made her feel "raped" and, as most of her experiences do, *"terminal"* (238). These memories are reproduced in Rennie's relationship with Paul, where the word "terminal" once again figures prominently. After she and Paul make love, Rennie drinks some "long-life milk" (238) and, back in bed, notices with appreciation that Paul has aged without showing signs of the deterioration that she experiences so poignantly in her own body. When Paul admits that he has been married, but could not settle down to a normal life, he confirms what Lora has told Rennie; he enjoys danger, the sensation of existing on the verge of being blown into "little pieces" (239). At the same time, he claims that he does not take risks, explaining to Rennie that that's why he remains "still alive" (239).

The conversation shifts and turns, first to dreams. In answer to Rennie's question about dreaming, Paul claims that he does not have time to dream. He then initiates an argument about women. Because he resents thinking of life as "issues," Paul dislikes the whole concept of Women's Lib; he argues that right and wrong, good and bad, are not absolute categories but shift in meaning according to the distribution of power. Both Nietzsche and Foucault would agree with his conviction that " 'there's only people with power and people without power. Sometimes they change places' " (240). Rennie's family, on the other hand, operated with absolute categories: "good girls" and "bad girls," the "decent" and the "indecent." Paul's lesson in semantics powerfully affects her; she acknowledges her inability to "predict men," admitting that she "used to think there was such a thing as most men, and now she doesn't" (241). She also admits that "she's given up deciding what will happen next" (241). Relinquishing her need to generalize and predict may be a necessary prelude to her rebirth.

The story continues, relocates, and we see other pictures. Paul stands in the kitchen with two fish, "one bright red, the other blue and green" (241); he holds a knife.[7] Once again, Rennie lies suspended in the hammock, thinking about "white light." "Cup-shaped" white flowers hang over the porch, while two "blue-green lizards" (241) watch. The sun sets. The conversation turns back to politics; the CIA is mentioned and connected with a game of suspicion. Rennie learns that Elva's box has been delivered to Paul who needs guns, and although part of her condemns him for being like a little boy playing with weapons, another part finds his renegade role romantic: "She can't help wondering whether Paul has any bullet holes in him. If he has, she'd like to see" (244). This kind of female voyeurism, we are meant to understand, encourages continued violence.

Even in spite of herself, then, Rennie is involved. We next find her, as if she were a prisoner, shut up in Paul's bedroom while a noisy meeting takes place in the living room. The election results have come in, and a group of men are negotiating their new positions. To escape from the background noise, Rennie, who still believes that the election has "nothing to do with her" (245), finds some Dell mysteries, their pages "yellowed and watermarked" and mouldy (245), and begins a game of guessing murderers and victims. She admits that she "doesn't have much patience for the intricacies of clues and deductions" (246). Perhaps here readers of *Bodily Harm* are being questioned about *their* reading habits, whether they pay enough attention to the novel's clues, whether they read patiently. The narrative also stresses a revealing disjunction. In one room, men argue election results; in another, a sole enclosed woman (once again, Rennie is alone), wishing that the men would "turn down the volume," figures out murderers and victims. About the latter, not surprsingly, Rennie guesses accurately: "two blondes with pale translucent skin, mouths like red gashes and swelling breasts" and "two tempestuous redheads," probably with oozing wounds "in the left breast." These clues imply that Rennie, wounded in the left breast, has become yet another victim while, at the same time, like Rennie, readers continue to have trouble pinning down the "murderers" (246).

When Paul returns to the bedroom, Rennie learns that Dr. Minnow has become the new Prime Minister, Prince, the Minister of Justice, and Marsdon, the Minister of Tourism. For the moment, Ellis seems to have lost. But when questioned, Paul admits his displeasure, for one reason because he thinks good men, like Minnow, pose hazards in politics. He claims that Minnow " 'believes in democracy and fair play and all those ideas the British left here along with cricket. . . . He thinks guns are playing dirty'" (247), although Dr. Minnow has earlier told Rennie that he had little admiration for the British. This contradiction suggests Paul's concern about his own illegal activities. Rennie has decided to leave the island the next day, and with what she imagines as "her last wish" (248), asks Paul again about his dreams. This time, his answer is chilling; he admits that he dreams "'about a hole in the ground'" (248). Once more, death faces us head on.

The action speeds up. Someone pounds at the door; Lora appears, dripping wet, sobbing, and bringing the news that Dr. Minnow has just been shot. For a moment, Rennie suspects a joke. But in fact, Dr. Minnow has been killed. The game board rearranges itself: "Dr. Minnow is in a closed coffin in the livingroom" (250), with the opened scissors emblematic of Ste. Agathe on top. Rennie mysteriously shows up in the room with the mourners in the middle of the night, where the occasion reminds her of her grandmother's funeral. People here sing in "three-part harmony" (250), as her mother and aunts did in Griswold, but on the island, the murdered man's widow cries openly, her face raw and naked. The attention to bodies makes Rennie conscious of her own; her legs have gone to sleep and the heat in the crowded room oppresses her. An ominous question and answer float through her mind: *What did she die of? Cancer, praise the Lord*" (251).

She goes outside where the men drink liquor while Marsdon harangues them. He wants action, and when she sees the machine gun in his hands, a frightened Rennie thinks about *"massive involvement"* (252). Paul tells her to return to his house and we next find Rennie and Lora moving in the dark through streets on which they can hear the sound of smashing glass and irregular gunfire. When "the underlying hum" stops — earlier, the "persistent hum" has been likened to a "heartbeat" (224) — Lora informs Rennie that the power plant has been taken; the lights go out. Since Ste. Agathe has only two policemen (we notice that there are always *two* policemen in this novel), the insurgents will take control of the police station. Although she has not been drinking or smoking dope, Rennie again feels "disoriented" (254). When the women get to the house, Paul is already there. Because Marsdon has just declared Ste. Agathe separated from St. Antoine, Paul wants Rennie and Lora to get off the island and, as he begins directing their escape, Rennie understands that he has suddenly come back to life. Another piece of the puzzle falls into place.

She thinks: "That's why we get into these messes: because they love it" (256). The women make their way to the dock, and when they arrive, Lora insists that they hide under it. Bars of shadow cast marks on them as the moonlight comes through the slats of the dock, and Rennie imagines telling Jocasta the story of their escape, even though so far the plot lacks excitement. But before they can leave for St. Antoine on the boat that Paul has brought, Marsdon, with a machine-gun and two of his men, stops them.

The focus shifts to a wooden table where Paul and Marsdon, equally matched with machine guns and rum, bargain. Rennie, who has become an "object of negotiation," feels "strangely uninvolved in her own fate. Other people are deciding that for her" (258). When Marsdon looks at her, his eyes gleaming in the moonlight, she imagines that he sees "fragmentation, dismemberment" (258). The story for Jocasta gathers suspense as events speed up, become increasingly confusing. Paul accuses Marsdon of being the new CIA agent, of setting up Prince and of killing Minnow. When she hears these accusations, Rennie automatically distances herself. The plot pauses while she "closes her eyes. Something with enormous weight comes down on them, she can hardly breathe" (259). The night sounds continue as before.

The rest of this section leads up to the final act. Back on St. Antoine after an hour and a half on the launch with Paul, Rennie feels sick. Once again, she is alone; Lora has decided to stay on Ste. Agathe with Prince, and Paul has left on the launch, its receding sound like "the drone of a summer insect" (260) blending with what seems to be a television cop show with the volume turned up. Although she tries to believe that everything is "normal" (261), when she gets back to the Sunset Inn, the Englishwoman, obviously gloating, tells her that the island's airport has been closed. Rennie returns to her room, where "she feels marooned" (261). Then, in yet another replay of the novel's opening break-in, the door of the motel room bursts open and two policemen enter with "grins, drawn guns" (262). They tell Rennie that they are arresting her on suspicion, and when she insists that she is simply a journalist, the designation sounds even to herself more and more unlikely. She thinks fleetingly of her empty note-book. As the policemen come forward, the Englishwoman looks at Rennie with pure enjoyment and the disembodied word *"Malignant"* (262) concludes the section.

Section Five seems considerably tighter than the four preceding sections; as a result, it also feels more threatening. Its imagery and themes emphasize competition. The opening paragraph presents Jake as a man who liked winning at sex, but with him, Rennie had begun to find this kind of competition profoundly threatening. Instead of a game, to her it seemed more like a war in which the enemies had been carefully drawn up and marked. Paul also enjoys the adrenalin rush he gets from competition, particularly if winning and losing are dangerous; he likes competing with Marsdon for control of the women. From a different perspective, Dr. Minnow is involved in the game of politics, a game in which winning and losing, as it becomes evident, can mean giving up one's life. The Englishwoman, and the two policemen at the end, in their own ways, apparently equate control over others with winning.

The frequent allusions to holes, the continued references to underground spaces and to textual gaps increase our sense of dislocation. The video of the rat emerging from a woman's vagina, shown to Rennie, illustrates confusions between internal and external boundaries, and suggests the imminent emergence of disgusting underground material. It also centers attention on women's bodies, drawing particular notice to holes. Other kinds of underground spaces emerge, for example the "hole in the ground" (248) dreamed of by Paul. Another in a series of suggested graves, such as the "raised oblong" (11) on the first page of the novel, this reference reminds us of the "hole" in Rennie's breast, and of her conviction that men are able to throw their darkness into women (into their "holes"). The underside of the dock recalls cellars, as well as other subterranean places. All imply a hellish journey. Dr. Minnow has been filled with holes from the gun that shot him, while his coffin (an enclosed space like the cabin of the launch and Rennie's motel room), like "an emblem out of some horrible little morality play" (250), contains a "history" with a "hole blown through it" (251). The potholes that Lora and Rennie step through to get away from trouble are filled with dirty water, while the landscape of Ste. Agathe, filled with heavy undergrowth, threatens captivity. The plot movement continues to be jerky, and jumps in time and space leave gaps in place of connections. Significantly, Rennie is becoming increasingly conscious of the spaces between what she used to think of as reality and what she now considers real.

Raw material, broken bodies, blood: throughout this section, bodies undergo all kinds of physical harm. The sculptor emphasizes the theme with his "female furniture," and the Police Department's pornography display continues it by displaying fetishized pieces of women's bodies. Rennie told Jake that he made her feel as if she were "raw material" (212), to be used, reconstructed, finished and discarded. Marsdon punishes his woman for her unfaithfulness by attacking her body. Elva appears with her face covered in blood, and Paul discusses, quite casually, the island custom of chopping up women. In the mysteries she finds in Paul's bedroom, Rennie discovers that the dead bodies are always women's, while the private eyes, always men, enjoy discussing "each detail of the body fully, lushly, as if running their tongues over it; all that flesh, totally helpless because totally dead" (246). As we move toward the final section of the novel, these themes and images weigh heavily on plot development, emphasize conflations of time and space, and turn characters into broken bodies.

PART SIX (CELLS)

As we begin the final section of *Bodily Harm*, we hear Lora's voice. She is talking about nationalism: " 'Anyone who'd die for their country is a double turkey as far as I'm concerned' " (265). She claims to have contempt for people who would sacrifice a life " 'for the good of all' " (265), even though, earlier, she had admitted loving Prince precisely because of his idealism. She talks about Prince's role in the current revolution, and reveals her belief that the whole set-up of the election and subsequent insurrection of Ste. Agathe's people has been a fortuitous excuse for men who like to play games, " 'sneaking around at night, having secrets, sort of like the Shriners' " (265).

While Lora talks, Rennie worries about her passport, currently (she thinks) in the safe at the Sunset Inn. At last, in this final section of the novel, Rennie lets us know where she and Lora are. They are "in here," in the army barracks/prison of Fort Industry, and Rennie hopes to be "let out" (267) in the morning. Lora slaps at the prison bugs and continues talking to Rennie about events on Ste. Agathe. St. Antoine's police stopped the revolution without much shooting by simply picking up anyone they found "hiding or running or even walking on the road" (267). Once they had the names of the main instigators of the uprising, they could easily extract the names of their relatives. On Ste. Agathe, "where everyone's related to everyone else" (267), that meant virtually all the people on the island. The prisoners were brought to St. Antoine, the men tied up in bundles with yellow nylon rope and dumped in the boat's hold "like they were cargo" (267); the women, with their hands tied together, were allowed to stand. On St. Antoine's dock, the crowd waiting for the prisoners shouted as if they were Roman soldiers for the prisoners to be killed, mostly because the radio had been calling them "communists." The prisoners were then taken to the main police station on St. Antoine, where about fifty or sixty men, tied together in a long line, were beaten up by the police. According to Lora, they used " 'sticks and boots, the works' " (267). The women were beaten up too, although not as severely.

Doused with cold water, the prisoners were jailed and Ellis, now in control again, announced a State of Emergency. Most of the people who have been imprisoned "don't have a clue" (268) as to why they were picked up; the police had suddenly broken into their houses and grabbed them. In spite of her own recent experiences, Rennie finds these events preposterous. Those who live in the midst of constant revolution do not. Lora points out the obvious, that people will believe whatever story the person in power wants to tell them, because questioning authority causes too much trouble. Furthermore, to underline the harm often perpetrated by uninformed foreign intervention, Lora explains that this small-time curtailed revolution will put Ellis in a position to request more foreign aid.

Again, the story shifts, pulls back. The narrator describes the setting for the conversation between Lora and Rennie: "The room they're in is about five feet by seven feet, with a high ceiling. The walls are damp and cool, the stone slick to the touch as if something's growing on it" (268). In this jail cell, we feel close to the heart of the story. The narrator evokes all of our senses. Here, Rennie dwells on the cold, the dampness of the stone floor, the bars on the door, the light shining in from the corridor outside. She notices the slogans "DOWN WITH BABYLON. LOVE TO ALL" (269) on the wall of the corridor, reminders of her earlier visit to Fort Industry; these ironically emphasize that now she too has become one of the women prisoners she met with Dr. Minnow. Through a small window at the top of the cell, Rennie and Lora see the moon. Inside the cell, a "bucket, red plastic" (269) recalls the red cup-like hibiscus flowers that grow all over the island and, forebodingly, the white basin that took on a reddish hue when filled with Elva's blood. Rennie wishes that " 'they'd turn out the lights' " (269) so that she can go to sleep, echoing similar desires expressed earlier in Rennie's and Jocasta's stories.

In this final section of the novel, we also realize that at least some of the stories that occur throughout are apparently being told by Rennie and Lora to each other, to help pass their time in the jail cell. The novel does not make clear at what point in the novel's present the stories supposedly begin, nor does it clarify exactly the relationship between those sections of Parts One to Five meant to be narrated, and those meant as unspoken memories. In Part Six, for the first time, Lora's stories are enclosed in quotation marks, and she does most of the storytelling. When Lora complains about Rennie's poor showing, Rennie admits to "having a hard time thinking up anything about her life that Lora might find interesting" (270). Earlier, she had imagined that Lora's stories would probably bore her, but now her own stories seem filled with ennui, as if, like the character of a book once lent to her by Jocasta, she has fallen off a cliff early in the plot, leaving the rest of the pages blank. Daniel had once told her to think of her life as a "clean page," but even then, Rennie had understood that empty was not "the same as clean" (84–85). Emptiness affects her now. When the conversation turns to rape, Rennie tells Lora about the man with the rope (we are back at the beginning of Part One), but Lora responds by describing her own actual rape. Rennie has again failed to tell the best story.

Scenes shift. As Lora talks, her mouth opening and closing (like that of a fish?), Rennie returns to voyeurism, imagining that she is watching a movie with the sound turned off. Lora picks up the movie analogy when she asks: " 'If it was two guys in here . . . you think they'd be talking about women? They'd be digging a tunnel or strangling the guards from behind. . . . Like at the movies' " (271). As the endless first night in the prison drags on, Rennie and Lora stay sitting up; the glaring light in the corridor keeps them awake.

Bored, Lora finally suggests that she lift Rennie up to the window high above. Rennie sees the courtyard Dr. Minnow had shown her and the gallows she had mistaken for a child's playhouse. She recognizes the "faint smell of pigs" (272). But the space is empty. Back on the floor with Lora, Rennie hears rats and tries to avoid thinking about her own "lack of power" (273). Instead, she contemplates the common objects often mentioned earlier in the novel: refrigerators, vacuum cleaners, bathtubs, beds. Beside her, on the cold floor, she senses Lora's arm. We suspect, too, that the detailed and frequent descriptions of food, often simple foods like milk and eggs, the bland foods served in hospitals, also reflect Rennie's hunger in the cell. Her discomfort reminds her of a time when she was trapped in a bus station during a blizzard, with a closed snack bar and broken toilets. Even the coffee machine was out of order. A woman "in a maroon coat and curlers" (273), on the bench beside her, kept talking to her, just as Lora does now, telling her about operations, sexual relationships, illnesses, "a web of blood relationships no one could possibly untangle." Rennie succeeds in tuning out the woman's *True Confessions*' "litany" (273) by concentrating on other stranded people in the station. In the jail cell, her only companion is Lora.

The expression "blood relationships" triggers Rennie's memory, and she is jolted back to the past where she walks on a street of red-brick houses with her mother and her grandmother. The season is Fall, and the three women are returning from church. Rennie feels ignored. When she looks for her hands, they are missing. She hears her grandmother's voice: "I don't want to die . . . I want to live forever" (274). Against the red leaves, the white of her grandmother's hat stands out. The night fills up the space around them.

As day returns to the cell and the sun through the prison window gets brighter, a policeman appears in the corridor. Another brings the women food, a slice of bread on a tin plate, a red bucket containing weak tea. The tea has salt in it. As the cell gets hotter, Rennie feels sweaty and claustrophobic. She smells the noxious fumes from the red pail on the floor. Like Lora's mother, who believed that if she kept hoping, she might get lucky, Rennie concentrates on rescue. Later, she tells herself that Paul will be trying to save both of them, although she understands that Paul may well be dead. Accompanied by two policemen, Lora gets the first chance to leave the cell; she takes the slop bucket out to empty it in "a hole in the ground" (276). When she returns, she has new details about the revolution, that Marsdon is dead, probably killed by Ellis, possibly by Paul. The general political instability and violence bewilder Rennie, while Lora, continuing and altering the game of Clue, claims the murderer's name to be unimportant. What matters is that the revolution appear real, not faked, because there is " 'nothing like a revolution to make the States piss money, and they've done it already. Canada just gave a great big lump of cash to Ellis' " (277). The islanders continue to assume that Rennie is a spy.

In the midst of apparent defeat, Lora believes that she has some control over her situation because the men guarding the women have sold drugs for her. More important, she knows that they were aware of the gun shipments from Colombia. Although Ellis probably would not mind the dealing, and could simply fire the two men if he did, he would have them killed if he found out that they knew about the guns. For the moment, Lora believes that this information will protect her from physical harm. She also trades sex for small favours that will make the time in jail more bearable and — her actual reason — to gain intelligence about Prince. But Rennie has become much less naïve than she was when she arrived on St. Antoine. She asks Lora the obvious question: " 'What's to stop them from just burying you quietly in the back yard?' " (279). Chillingly perceptive, this question foretells the future.

The day wears on; here, time is more specifically marked than in earlier sections, often by the arrival of meals. Once again feeling nauseous, Rennie gives her food (cold rice and partly cooked chicken) to Lora, but by suppertime, the women are not speaking. Rennie feels herself to be "deteriorating" (280) and although, earlier, Lora had insisted that " 'where there's life there's hope' " (279), she too appears dirty and thinner, with "dark moons" (281) under her eyes and a sore that will not heal on her leg. The raw, bitten flesh around her nails becomes more noticeable. Rennie conjures up images of fast-food, and we remember Paul's observation that what one eats depends on what one has for food. Rennie tries putting together an imaginary jigsaw puzzle with a "pure blue" (280) sky, like the sky that appears in her dreams of her grandmother. Finally, she asks Lora about her dreams. Lora has no trouble answering. She tells Rennie that she dreams about her mother and about having babies and this response draws the women closer. Rennie does Lora's hair and, for the first time in the novel experiencing closeness to another woman, imagines them cleaning each other's faces with the weak tea.

As in every section thus far, Rennie's physical boundaries fluctuate.

The border between sleeping and waking remains hazy, and verb tenses mingle with each other. The dead and the living walk together. But in this final section of the story, Rennie attempts to make sense out of her life. To do so, she needs to concentrate on plot and work through the radical split that still affects her. When she tries to order the story's sequence into past, present and future, she feels most "at home" in the past because "the present is both unpleasant and unreal; thinking about the future only makes her impatient, as if she's in a plane circling and circling an airport, circling and not landing" (282–83). The image of the plane, to be used again shortly, effectively describes Rennie's sense of suspension, the parenthetical nature of both time and space. Nonetheless, as the novel draws to its conclusion, Rennie begins to want active control of her life. She cannot imagine existing permanently in fear; she "wants an end" (283) and this desire, no longer a passive need for rescue, means reorganizing time toward some point.

To begin this process, she focusses on love, initially meaning her relationships with men. Her sexual connection with Jake, however, has left only "a change, a result, a trace, hand through the sea at night, phosphoresence." All she can conjure up of Paul are the "too-blue eyes." Daniel hardly seems tangible. She thinks of him "in surgery, a body spread before him, his hands poised for incision" (283), the man who has told her that she was "alive" (284), the man encased in a "glass bubble." Rennie remains "on the outside looking in," where all that matters is that "nothing has happened to her yet, nobody has done anything to her, she is unharmed" (284). Thus, she comes to grips with one fact about death, that other people are dying faster (and a good deal more unpleasantly) than she is herself. The nighttime screams give voice to this revelation.

When she opens her eyes and returns to the jail cell, she hears a buzzing. Caused by the wasps on the ceiling of the cell, this sound echoes the noises of the plane's air conditioner, the dream hummingbirds, the ceiling fans common in the islands, the hum of the power plant and, of course, the overhead unit in the hospital. Caught up in this sound, Rennie at last places herself as the anonymous narrator of *Bodily Harm*: "Pretend you're really here, she thinks. Now: what would you do?" (284). What she would do if she were really in this Caribbean jail under threat of death as a spy forces her into a new situation as writer/narrator, one quite different from her writing as a life-styles journalist. Rennie must distance herself from the group referred to by Lora as " '*women like you*' " (286) and become knowledgeable about the actualities of torture.

Thus, she reflects on a disturbingly real pain. We are back inside her body; doubled over and crouching, sweaty and dizzy, Rennie fights against invasion, betrayal. We feel the cold floor of the jail cell. Rennie's head swells; it resembles the picture of the opened watermelon on the wall of the Sunset Inn, the unpleasant split-open husks in the Lime Tree's garden. Overcome with thirst, she believes death to be close. Cancer and torture intertwine, as Rennie questions the rationale of suffering: "What has she done, she's not guilty, this is happening to her for no reason at all" (286). Luck takes on new meaning, and so does control. As she struggles with plot, Rennie returns to media images she has used frequently before, imagining tuning down the loud screaming she hears in the distance so that she can sleep. We are again assured that "no one has done anything to her yet" (287). She dreams. We swing back to the opening segment of the novel, to the man with the rope. Now, the man is with her, faceless, then cloned, assuming the faces of Jake pretending to be a rapist, of Daniel with his surgeon's knife in hand, and of Paul who had effaced himself with mirror sunglasses. And then, another revelation. Rennie understands that the faceless man is none other than a "shadow," both "anonymous" and familiar" (287), a silver-eyed twin of Rennie herself. Somewhat different from the dreams of her grandmother but, like it, offering clues, this revelation marks another step towards Rennie's acknowledgement of responsibility. Masculinity and femininity are twinned. Get rid of one concept, you remove the other.

As Part Six proceeds, time closes in and the prison scenario plays itself through. We are told that Rennie's "life is shrinking right down to that one sound, a dull bell" (288), the sound of bones being scraped into the red bucket. Background screams continue as she focusses again on the prison's courtyard. This time, she sees the police, armed with sticks and cattle prods, disciplining some androgynous figures who turn out to be men. One of the policemen chases a terrified pig with a cattle prod. Another raises a rifle, seems about to shoot, detaches the bayonet and walks behind the group of men. Rennie understands, probably for the first time, the pleasures and power of torture. The word *"malignant"* recurs, and Rennie imagines "butchery" (289) although, instead of cutting throats, the policeman begins to cut the prisoners' hair. The courtyard becomes a picture; silent, with the sun beating down, everything glistens with sweat. The hair-cutting ceremony seems as "precise as an operation" (289) and Rennie sees blood. She turns up the volume again. The man who has been cut howls, is kicked, has a cattle prod jammed between his legs. An inhuman scream resounds. As she watches, Rennie sees that the bleeding man is none other than the deaf and dumb man "who has a voice but no words" (290) and, as he did when he was beaten by the police earlier, he looks directly into her eyes. The expression *"oh please"* appears, as usual, from nowhere.

Giving narrative perspective to such material is not easy. Shaking, Rennie now understands what Dr. Minnow meant when he told her that nothing was "inconceivable" in certain political situations. The composite image of the man with the rope resolves itself, comes into focus. And Rennie understands: "She's afraid of men and it's simple, it's rational, she's afraid of men because men are frightening" (290). Moreover, her own complicity has become clear. Unable any longer to separate "here" from "there," the space that she inhabits from the rest of the world, inside from outside, she accepts responsibility. She acknowledges that "this is not necessarily a place she will get out of, ever. She is not exempt. Nobody is exempt from anything" (290). Once Rennie has understood Amnesty International's message, that all humanity is linked, that what happens in one part of the world affects every other part, she has begun to comprehend subversion.

Working through this knowledge becomes another matter. The plot continues. Now, the guards come to the cell, and one of them demands that Rennie, rather than Lora, accompany them. But the new guard, a replacement for the old one whose "grandmother got sick" (291), tells Lora of Prince's death. This confession dramatically affects the plot's direction. The guard's inadvertent honesty contradicts the rules of the game as played by those in power; it uncovers the scrim. For a moment, the exposure is caught, held still. And then everything moves again. Lora attacks, hysterically threatening to expose one of the guard's activities. When she tries to kick his groin, both guards attack her, going for "the breasts and the buttocks, the stomach, the crotch, the head" (293). During this scene, Rennie reaches a crisis; she "wants to tell them to stop. She wants to be strong enough to do that but she isn't, she can't make a sound, they'll see her. She doesn't want to see, she has to see, why isn't someone covering her eyes?" (293). In this visually oriented text, eyes, as we have discovered, assume different meanings ranging from voyeurism to multiple perspectives. So too does silence. As in the silence of dreams, and the many references to turning down or off media volume, Rennie's muteness implies separation, uninvolvement, paralysis. This extended crisis of conscience brings Rennie to further recognitions. Although forced upon her by circumstances and, in spite of what her Griswold background might tell her, not her fault, in spite of her neutrality as a Canadian, in spite of her femininity, in spite of her role as travel writer, her involvement becomes real.

The rest of the novel, cast into the simple future tense, has perplexed many readers. "This is what will happen" (293). I suggest that, having arrived at this critical moment in her account of what she would do if she were really in this situation, Rennie is faced with several possible conclusions, the most simple of which would be her rescue. Such an ending, conventional to fairy-tales and romances, might show her being taken out of the cell to a small, apple-green room, with a calendar with a "sunset" on it, where a comforting policeman (an "older man with short greying hair" [293]) would ask her to sign a statement that she has suffered no bodily harm in prison. To use this ending, Rennie would have to forget about Lora. She tries it out. She agrees to sign the form, asks to change her clothes, is taken to a room where another calendar displays a "white woman in a blue bathing suit" (294) and, when she sees her own clothes, begins to cry. Emerging dressed in a faded blue-cotton dress, with her suitcase and purse, she is startled by the spaciousness of the room to which she is taken, and remembers that here crafts were to be sold. Her trip to Fort Industry now seems part of a different life and, of course, Dr. Minnow is dead. In the room, the representative from the Canadian government waits for her, still in his safari-jacket and tinted sun-glasses. He wants Rennie to understand that the political situation is returning to normal.

As she constructs this ending, Rennie realizes that such a rescue could function only at the expense of honesty. She must agree to be silent. The man tells her that the incident is "regrettable" (294), that journalists should not be imprisoned. But he also emphasizes Rennie's suspected subversion. We understand that she continues to be held hostage because he does not want another Grenada on his hands.

When she looks out the window and sees the flashing silver of a plane "up there in the viciously blue air" (296), Rennie recognizes rescue. The "superman" ending has many appeals.

But it does not work. Rennie has to return to Lora, to the suspended crisis in the prison cell. Now alone with Lora's body, which is lying on the floor, massively mutilated, Rennie thinks: *What if she's dead*? (296). A new victim has been added to the novel's board game; answers are not forthcoming. The corridor remains "empty and silent" (297).

Another jump, much farther into the past. Rennie is now back in her grandmother's kitchen, where a soft noise (the radio? the television?) fills the air. Her grandmother, in a black dress covered with white flowers, comes through a door, looking for her hands. Rennie backs away from her and, as her grandmother starts to cry, Rennie's mother enters. Disgusted with Rennie for not remembering what to do, she carefully puts down her groceries, turns, and clasps her mother's hands in her own.

The memory of this episode gives Rennie the necessary emotional information to continue with the story of the body in the jail cell. Taught by her mother and her grandmother, Rennie looks at Lora's hands shining, translucent; the rest of the body is in darkness. Turning it over, Rennie sees only bruised pulp where the face used to be and admits that "it's the face of a stranger, someone without a name, the word *Lora* has come unhooked and is hovering in the air" (298). Like a photograph, the scene stays still, then shifts to moving picture. Rennie, holding Lora's hand, begins to pull Lora through "an invisible hole in the air" (299). She hears herself moaning. This image of birth from death announces Rennie's realization that the ending she has first imagined has not been complete. She has been changed. The words " 'Oh God' " (299), whether from her mouth or Lora's, imply conversion.

Rennie returns to the plot's conclusion. Now she can imagine herself on an airplane, in Toronto, even alone, but she must include her new awareness of struggle. Superimposed on the pictures in the airplane's *Leisure* magazine, is the "shape of a hand in hers, both of hers, there but not there, like the afterglow of a match that's gone out. It will always be there now" (300). The objects and events of the world have not changed, but Rennie's perspective has. And with this change, Rennie feels that her body has been returned to her, as if from somewhere in the future. What would you do? She illustrates her changed perspective by refusing to pretend to be a tourist. She has lost her ability to construct snappy epigraphs, flashy titles. For what she has imagined and remembered, she cannot think of any title at all. When the man beside her on the plane asks her to dinner, she chooses, from a list of possibilities, to tell him the truth, that "she doesn't have enough time, she has to meet a deadline." Unlike her customary response, designed to flatter men's egos, this answer reveals that, at last, she has become "subversive" (301).

Alone, she looks out of the plane's window, but instead of the suspensions that she has described throughout, moments of time in which her head seems severed from her body, now she imagines herself solid, tangible, whole. Beneath her, she looks at the sea, some islands, the shadow of the plane, while inside, chilled from the air conditioning, she feels the scar on her breast. Like the imprint of Lora's hand, it too will be with her always, "a reminder, a silent voice counting, a countdown." She understands and, more important, accepts the fact that she "doesn't have much time left" (301). The proximity of death forces her to pay attention. As Rennie constructs this ending, then, she perceives that by no longer waiting to be saved, she has saved herself. She assumes responsibility for her life and accepts the concept of luck. Unlike earlier versions of *Bodily Harm*'s conclusion, where the plane touches the ground at the end, Atwood finally chose to conclude with Rennie imagining herself suspended in the air.

Section Six replays all the imagery of the novel, showing how sado-masochism affects personal and public lives alike. Men fight, whether for country or women, absorbing violence as if it were a hard drug. At first, the scenarios imagined seem as flat and distanced as video games; just as Lora says, about the men involved in Ste. Agathe's revolution: " 'The truth is I thought they were just having a good time' " (265). But Rennie learns that violence and pleasure are intimately linked and because of this linkage, she can never again look condescendingly at, or participate in, men's games. She has to give up masochism, sadism's twin. Indeed, all the strands of the plot, like the people on the islands, seem related to something else. Ropes, used to tie up the insurgents, recall the man with the rope and, more imagistically, the tying up of loose ends undertaken by Rennie. A man wants to tie Lora to the bedpost, and the woman Rennie meets at the bus station describes a "web of blood relationships" (273). Even the image of the "jigsaw puzzle" (280), made up of its interlocking pieces, seems a metaphor for the novel's segments, which the reader must piece together.

Tensions between exposure and deceit also figure prominently in this closing section. Paul explains to Marsdon that the revolution is bound to fail because police helicopters, circling the hills, will pick up the insurgents: " 'there's no cover up there, it's just scrub' " (266). Without a passport, Rennie feels "naked" (267). After the beating of prisoners, the new Justice Minister covers up by announcing that no violence has occurred, that "the people got the cuts and bruises from falling down when they were running away" (268). The prison guards do not want Lora to blow their cover, and when Rennie imagines the prison-leaving scene, she recognizes the Canadian representative's embarrassment about the possible uncovering of what happens at Fort Industry. When he says, "we can't interfere in internal matters" (295), jail cells and cancer cells eerily intertwine. During the course of her operation, Rennie's cover has been destroyed; she has been opened up.

INTERPRETING *BODILY HARM*

In the Atwood archives, along with typescripts of various pieces for *Murder in the Dark*, appears a short prose piece entitled "Inter/view: Considering R." (Box 69). About the construction of a character called Rennie, the segments of this short piece reveal an author in the process of composition. The characters she creates seem both to have a life of their own and to be entirely subject to the writer's will. For example, discussing Rennie, the writer discloses that "a couple of paces behind her there's a man, who either does or does not have a gun — nobody knows yet, including me — and he's also frozen in time, with one foot, probably the left, slightly in the air as well. I can tell you that the man is wearing boots and Rennie is not"; the writer later admits that "Rennie is still in the air. I haven't been able to get back to her. She's feeling no pain because she's feeling no time, everything is just as it was." Apart from showing the half-lives of literary characters, the piece also demonstrates the desire of reviewers and critics to discover from authors what their novels *really* mean.

In "Inter/view," the writer admits, ironically, that "it's a week later and nothing has changed for R. She's still on that tropical hill and I'm still in Toronto, Ontario. . . . The young woman sitting across from me is a journalist, ambitious, thirty. She wants the real story. Apparently what I have to say isn't real enough for her." The piece concludes by showing the writer's returning creativity. Sitting in a room, she sees that

> behind the pink tree, out of sight but behind it, is the hill with the path where Rennie still stands, where Rennie still stands. Suddenly it's night, a black space punctured above by stars, around us by fireflies and the bell notes of whatever's hiding in the trees. There's fear here, violence is somewhere, not only in the man who may or may not have a gun but ahead, behind. No one knows what will happen next, but something will, because I'm back here finally, a soul returning to a body, this is real, questions have been left behind and there's no real need for answers. I stretch out my hand and Rennie begins to move.

As a kind of gloss on *Bodily Harm*, these segments are revealing. I quote them as another clue towards a reading of this ambiguous novel. Apart from humorously demonstrating authorial control, they echo the third-person sections of *Bodily Harm*, in which the narrator moves the characters as if they were pieces on a game-board. Repeatedly, too, in *Bodily Harm*, as I have emphasized in my reading, time and space are profoundly confusing, compressed. Movement in time, as it more obviously is in *Cat's Eye*, where the narrator "began then to think of time as having a shape, something you could see, like a series of liquid transparencies, one laid on top of another" (CE 3), seems to be movement through space. These segments also reveal a threatening, not quite locatable, violence, a hostility that infuses the very air the characters breathe. Although guns and boots suggest danger from men, the whole landscape exudes fear. *Bodily Harm* repeatedly evokes just such free-floating danger.

The piece also emphasizes the "inter/view," alluding not only to the conversation taking place between a journalist who wants the "real story" and a writer who cannot respond, but also to the fact that the segments represent alternative ways of seeing, and occur in different times and spaces. The writer works in a room in Toronto, where she creates the landscape, for example the "tropical hill" and the "pink tree," that emerge as the island setting of *Bodily Harm*. The island's remoteness from Canada, where the story is being written, also emphasizes contrasting angles of vision. Furthermore, the writer likens the experience of composition to that of having a soul return to a body. Throughout *Bodily Harm*, Rennie frequently imagines her body to be emptied out, flat, like a paper cut-out. But in certain places, junctures take place; Rennie's soul joins her body. Then, the character fills out, thickens, coheres. One of the novel's most dramatic moments occurs when Rennie imagines pulling Lora through an invisible hole in the air. Connected with the moment of intercourse with Paul, when Rennie imagines entering her body again, or, earlier, when she sees her body on a table and wants to rejoin it but is unable to "get down" (173), this struggle, this creation, seems the "hardest thing she's ever done" (299).

To interpret the novel, we also need to pursue the metaphor of Clue. The Detective notes for the game list suspects (Colonel Mustard, Professor Plum, Mr. Green, Mrs. Peacock, Miss Scarlett, Mrs. White), weapons, and rooms. Certainly, the characters do not blatantly reenact the game, although Rennie almost always wears white, Lora seems a scarlet woman, and Jocasta dresses like a peacock. The novel is filled with weapons, spaces are carefully delineated, and the author repeatedly points us toward the game as we read. She presents the opening episode as one of the combinations in the game, although a naïve Rennie, who really does not play well, confuses the names of the characters and admits that she does not know "whether the name in the envelope was supposed to be the murderer's or the victim's." She constructs a combination based on the rope left on her bed: *"Miss Wilford, in the bedroom, with a rope"* (14). Other combinations are either mentioned or implied: "the doctor, in the hospital, with the knife"; "the Englishwoman, in the Sunset Hotel, with the knife" (this version appears in Atwood's notes, Archives, Box 34); "the guards, in the jail cell, with the guns/boots"; and a more general one, which reflects "Inter/view," "the author, in the text, with the pen."

How does using the game of Clue help us read *Bodily Harm*? Apart from emphasizing that interpretation involves collecting and reading clues (Rennie demonstrates many of the problems that occur when clues are ignored or falsely read), the metaphor also draws attention to the games people play and, ironically, to the common conjunction

between violence and sport. For example, the policemen who investigate the break-in treat Rennie as if she were a participant in some
hoax initiated by a game-playing intruder. Perhaps unwittingly, Jake
disguises his sadism as a game in which one of the rules requires
Rennie's passivity, her masochism. The Toronto pornography
exhibit presents objects and pictures as sexual games. Paul plays with
guns, enjoying the power of violence and the ability to move "pieces"
around the "board." The prison guards revel in their control of other
human beings whom they treat like objects; just before beating Lora
senseless, one of them laughs about the fact that another has tricked
her into sexual intercourse by telling her that Prince was in the prison:
" 'You tell her you got him in here, make her work hard for you, eh?
Get some for your own self. You are a bad man.' He's laughing now,
not just giggling, this is the funniest thing he's heard in a long time"
(292).

Thus, Atwood demonstrates that treating sexual relationships as
games can result in terrible damage, notably by encouraging sado-
masochistic practices in other pursuits. Prison discipline, police
structures, and politics all reflect sexual perversion. By encouraging
voyeurism, sado-masochism insists on a division between the observer and the observed, a division that has conventionally assumed
gender characteristics; women watch as passive observers of active
male game-players. In political and cultural situations, the passivity
of the colonized often encourages extended and violent colonization.
As Dr. Minnow says about the Grenadines: "The Cubans are building a large airport in Grenada. The CIA is here, they wish to nip
history in the bud, and the Russian agents. It is of general interest to
them" (135).

The game of Clue and the short "Inter/view" suggest a reading of
Bodily Harm not usually pursued. In a 1982 conversation with
Margaret Atwood that followed my first reading of *Bodily Harm*,
Atwood mentioned to me that the novel's action takes place in a few
hours. I have often thought about this remark. Except for some very
early critiques of the novel, which tended to ignore the first sentence
and to accept the novel as a straightforward recital of events, most
critics have recognized the importance of storytelling, and have
accepted as the "here" of the novel the jail cell in Fort Industry. Other
critics, while stressing this narrative space, go on to argue that Rennie
survives her ordeal in order to write about her experiences. Let me

suggest another, not necessarily exclusive, possibility, that Rennie never leaves the hospital room where she is undergoing an operation for cancer. We are, of course, dealing with fiction. But the jail-cell reading has never entirely explained certain problems about duration and location, for example, the number of days Lora and Rennie remain incarcerated, the point at which the stories begin and stop, the perspective of the verb "would" ("what would you do?" [284]), and the meaning of the controlling narrative consciousness that speaks of Rennie in the third person.

Nor has this reading adequately accounted for the hospital images evoked on almost every page. Clothing, for example, replicates the uniforms of doctors and nurses; the Canadian government official wears a white safari jacket, the waitresses in the Caribbean and the stewardesses on the airplane appear in pastel uniforms. Rennie almost always wears white, "a plain white cotton dress" (59), a "white shirt and wrap skirt, also white" (203). The food described — flat gingerale, "alien vegetables," "lime Jello" (43), bread and butter, grapefruit juice, cheese sandwiches, weak tea, biscuits, partly cooked chicken — is innocuous and plain. Beds are made with "hospital corners" (203) and noises, notably one above Rennie's head, suggest an operating room. So does the reiterated attention to hands and to masked figures. Rennie frequently relives the sensation of receiving anaesthetic. Her fantasies of leaving the jail cell replicate a patient's discharge from a hospital.

I suggest, then, to quote words from one of the epigraphs Atwood considered using, from Seltzer's *Mortal Lessons*, that this novel searches for "some meaning in the ritual of surgery," a meaning at once "murderous, powerful, healing, and full of love." Throughout each section of the novel, the reader suffers with Rennie an incision that leads to greater political awareness. So, in Part One, apparently at the Sunset Inn (sunsets suggest death), Rennie, semi-conscious, feels "clogged and furry," senses something moist pressing down on her mouth, and sees a pulsing dot that suggests the flashing of a cardio-vascular machine. She imagines that she may have screamed, and suffers pain in her left shoulder. Elsewhere, she hears a woman's voice, apparently raised in agony, and expressions like "painful," "severed from her," and "get it over" evoke hospital conversation and thoughts. She experiences what she hears as an "intrusion" (49). In the novel, these sensations, occurring supposedly on St. Antoine, may be memories of the operation caused by the similar circumstances of the jail cell. But they seem strikingly immediate.

And so the stories proceed, frequently interrupted by what I have called suspended states. At the end of Part Two, again in her motel room, Rennie gratefully smokes dope to relax. She imagines what the x-rays of cancerous tissue look like, showing up "hot orange under one kind of light, hot blue under another," and senses her good cells dividing in the darkness, while the bad cells multiply with "furious energy." As she does in many other places in the novel, she checks herself, deciding that she is "still alive" (100). As if overhearing comments made around her during an operation, she notes words like "visible, soft, penetrable" (102), imagines herself on a bed with "no clothes on," and recalls (ostensibly with Jake) being asked to put her hands over her head so that her breasts would be lifted. At the end of the section, Rennie repeats the expressions "open up" and "opens you up" (106).

The three-part dream sequence in Section Three (115–16) moves toward some temporal location, perhaps in response to the novel's opening sentence. In the first and second parts of it, Rennie concentrates on hands, as one, half-conscious, might do during an operation. At first, she sees herself stretching out her hands toward her dead grandmother; the figure is insubstantial, and Rennie's hands pass through it. Then she imagines the loss of her own hands, possibly because they are held down during surgery. While experiencing these connected dreams, Rennie vaguely notes her surroundings: the whirring noise overhead, the grey window, the dim room. She tells us that she wears a white gown with ties at the back, although she insists that she is not in a hospital. She has been separated from her clothes, which have been put away in a bureau. In the first segment of the dream, she feels cold. In the third, the air, warm and misty, encloses Rennie just as the mosquito netting does. This last segment takes place "here," a place that is apparently the "future" of the former parts of the dream. She is (and this point seems important) by herself, and wants to get back to the past, probably the garden of the first part of the dream.

The fourth section focuses on the hospital room. Rennie, caught between waking and sleeping, imagines part of herself (third person? narrator?) up on the ceiling, observing the body (first person? character?) below. The observer hovers somewhere close to the humming air-conditioner and can "see everything, clear and sharp, under glass" (172). The body, covered with a green cloth, lies on an operating table, and the figures around it wear masks. We hear the words "performance," "procedure," and "incision," and the masked, faceless figures probe deeply toward the heart. Rennie assumes that "possibly her life is being saved" (173), although she seems unable to join her body. Such a division, as I have implied, helps explain the peculiar splits between the first and third person narrations, and the sensation that readers share of somehow remaining at all times within Rennie's control.

At the end of Part Four, another duplicitous event occurs. Ostensibly, Rennie describes intercourse with Paul, but her choice of phrases seems odd and the underlying themes peculiarly evocative of an operation. Rennie now insists that she accepts the idea of not living forever, and because she does, understands differently the significance of touching. Hands assume further resonances. Then, as if returning to the situation described in the hospital room in Part Three, Rennie repeats the sensation of being opened and, as if a step further along in a procedure, being "drawn back down" so that she can "[enter] her body again." She acknowledges the moment of juncture as painful, and tells us that the pain may suggest a "last clutch at the world" (204) before she slides towards death. This peculiar, sexual moment, then, the sensation of being touched, of feeling hands upon her, may mean that she has survived part of the operation.

In Section Five, apparently once again in bed with Paul, Rennie describes him as a "shape in the darkness, above her" (217). Another man, with something "white, a stocking or a gauze bandage" (217) has joined them in the bed. Somewhere outside the room, Rennie hears a hymn and the uneasy sound of bleating. A little later, the "faceless stranger" (233) touches her again. At another point, Rennie struggles to find a body, Paul's, "beneath the tangible one" (222), senses "a persistent hum," a "throb, a steady heartbeat" (224), concentrates on women who have been sliced or chopped, feels sick from the "sight of blood in the white basin" (230), thinks of the words "normal" (231), "terminal" (233), and *massive involvement* (234), sees herself in a "well-lit visible frozen pose at the kitchen table" (236), imagines oozing wounds in women's left breasts, and describes coffins and holes in the ground. In the "grey-white light"

(256), she is "disoriented" (254), concentrates on "fragmentation, dismemberment" (258), feels something "with enormous weight" (259) come down on her eyes and, as Part Five ends, imagines herself to be in the middle of a "bad dream" (262).

The final section of the novel concentrates on enclosure and physical discomfort. In this section, Rennie alternates between being too cold and too hot; she "doesn't feel too well" (279), and believes that she may be "deteriorating" and, possibly, "delirious" (280). She notices raw flesh. Past, present, and future level out, although her fatigue and fear suggest the need for chronology, a progress towards an "end" (283). She imagines her doctor, Daniel, in a "glass bubble" (she has earlier portrayed her own body under glass) and, listening to the sound overhead (the continuation of life-support systems?), understands that "nothing has happened to her yet" (284). Again, she mentions screams, and admits that she "may be dying" (284). In one place, as I have suggested above, she points to the construction of stories as a device; "Pretend you're really here" (284), she says and thereafter constructs the fictional "here" of the prison cell, a space aptly constituted to "explain" her pain, her body's betrayal. There, she can pay attention to various sensations, the sweat "dripping down her back," the perception of "swelling up" (286), of bursting open, her terrible thirst. She hears the statement " 'you'll live' " (287). In another passage, the male characters of the novel merge into one who, enclosed in glass, reflects her own eyes. During the novel's most critical episode, Rennie imagines pulling Lora through an "invisble hole in the air" (299), but it is probably the moaning of her own voice that she actually hears. Thus, when she says, "something will move and live again, something will get born" (299), we understand, partly because her first name means rebirth, that Rennie is being born. She will survive this operation.

CONCLUSION

I consider *Bodily Harm* to be the most carefully structured of Margaret Atwood's novels and politically, the most profound and radical. I have suggested a reading that encourages us to accept the whole of the multi-layered narrative as contained within Rennie's consciousness. Memories, personal stories, and constructed plot mingle. The stories structured to appear as if told by Rennie and Lora, include some memories, projection (the tales of the man with the rope, the break with Jake, the affair with Daniel, the last lunch with Jocasta), and Lora's narrations. The constructed plot is the island story, made up of "characters" connected with people Rennie has known, and with familiar "dialogue." After all, Rennie is a writer. The island plot comes to its crisis in the sixth section where memory, narration, and plot unite. In this section, the point of *Bodily Harm* becomes clear. The process of being opened up has helped Rennie understand political commitment, and has made her sensitive to the fact that terrorism, torture, and political upheaval *can* touch people, even when they live in Canada. In the final section, she comes to grips with the possibility of her own subversive action against the politics of terrorism. This recognition represents a political rebirth that parallels Rennie's operation for cancer, an operation that, while it may not have stopped the cancer,[8] has extended her life.

Hospital rooms and jail cells have many similarities. Silence, invisibility, dis/ease, opening, holes, and cells relate to both. Most interpretations of *Bodily Harm* choose the jail cell, showing how Rennie and Lora exchange stories with each other as they wait to be judged, killed, or rescued. Lora and Rennie may be distinct characters, although I confess to finding the similarities between them odd, as if Lora were a sort of lower-class Rennie, the indecent version who has turned her back on middle-class Griswold. Throughout the novel, Rennie repeatedly assures us that she is alone, so that I choose, rather, to interpret Rennie's dialogue with Lora as the working out of Rennie's own political conscience and Lora as a character constructed by Rennie so that she can dramatize redemption. My reading emphasizes connections between autobiography and politics. I am mindful, nonetheless, of Blaise's objection that, in *Bodily Harm*, "the Caribbean material is not wholly integrated to the text (as the intrusive reminders from cancer terminology serve to make clear), and that dangerous literary conceits are being played in running the twin tales of despoilment together" (112); and Tiffin's to the novel's "monocultural perspective" (121). Have I made more or less persuasive *Bodily Harm*'s serious charges about trade relations between Canada and Central America, about the support given by the United States to drug trafficking and gun running, and about British callousness to the political plights of former colonies?

I have stressed Rennie's representability. On one level, I would argue that Rennie stands for people living in countries apparently removed from internal terrorist threat. Such people are not easily "opened up"; the media has made them voyeurs of third-world violence, and "outrage" seems a too extreme response to what they read and see. On another, more limited level, Rennie initially represents youngish, unattached women, more superficial than many, but less superficial than some. When she develops cancer, she changes. Reviewers and critics of this novel often treat Atwood's detailed presentation of the struggle with cancer as a trivial issue. I do not agree. Rennie comes to represent women, like Jennifer Rankin for example, who have contracted breast cancer. For these women, this disease is not a minor glitch in a life's trajectory. Profoundly debilitating, it causes physical, psychological, moral, and spiritual crises. In *Bodily Harm*, the effects of this face-to-face combat transform Rennie from someone who, like many of us, focusses on life's superficial issues, to a person who pays attention to complex problems and develops thereby a political conscience. For however long she will live, it stands to reason that her journalistic career will undergo a massive shift. She will, in the future, pay attention to world problems, rather than to the covering "scrim." Davidson rightly points to the novel's central theme as "confrontation" (7). Does it matter where confrontation occurs, provided it does? Through her existential struggle with death, Rennie becomes everywoman and, finally, every person.

This novel demonstrates the transformation of the ignorant. If even the most superficial of people can be "opened up," if people in so-called "neutral" countries like Canada can be touched, if the most trivial journalism can be infected with the recognition of suffering, then the messages of organizations like Amnesty International have not gone unheeded. As long as one's own skin is safe, the horror stories that emerge from Central and South America seem distant, exaggerated, even hysterical. Torture fails to move us. But such a detailed examination of a "flayed" body, "untangled / string by string" (TS 51), should. *Bodily Harm*'s gross physicality dramatizes torture in ways that intellectual theorizing does not, and that so-called civilized codes of "niceness" and "decency" cannot. Unlike *Life Before Man*, in which Nate's mother is too peripheral of a character to make her social conscience a moral standard of the fictional world,

Bodily Harm centres political commitment and reflects North America's belated awakening to torture in El Salvador, to the disappeared in Argentina. Atwood has placed the "sweet Canadians" at the centre of this novel. In Canada, Rennie has her political rebirth, and in Canada she will be called forth to speak. She never loses her Canadian voice. And as a North American, a Canadian, it would, according to Atwood, be "simple stupidity" to assume that Rennie is "exempt" (SW 332). As Northrop Frye assures us Atwood is, Canadians must be "constantly aware that a few hours away on a plane there are police states where all the serious writers have been jailed or killed as a matter of perverted principle" (Archives Box 7).

Other information in the Atwood archives makes clear that Atwood listened to people talking when she visited the Caribbean, and studied the development of the British islands. She even wrote some of *Bodily Harm* and *True Stories* there (*Chateleine*, May 1982, 44). In a 1983 conversation conducted by Francis Gillen, she claimed that politics and art do not exist in separate boxes, and pointed to the work of Carolyn Forché as an example of how "political engagement can give a writer tremendous energy" (VanSpanckeren 241). In a 1988 interview, she agreed that " 'it would be very nice to live in a world in which politics was not necessary,' " but since clearly such is not the case, " 'the choice we have is ignore it and let the politicians do what they like, or pay attention and scream' " (Kirchhoff C13). Rennie becomes the mouthpiece for a developing conscience. In the novel's world, although she may never get to the islands of the Caribbean, she tells us that she and Jake visited Mexico. There, she tried hard not to *see* what was happening, but many scenes and images stayed with her and seem to be restructured in the story that takes place on the imaginary islands of Ste. Agathe and St. Antoine. As she comes to terms with what torture means, she at last discovers that no one is exempt from responsibility for other human beings. Most important, as she is "opened up," Rennie comes to understand that the sado-masochistic game playing in which she and Jake have indulged, the attitudes of police forces, even the "patient" game she imagines playing with her doctor, are psychologically linked to terrorism and torture.

Bodily Harm is, then, a profound statement about human responsibility and suffering; we are, this novel insists, our sisters' (and brothers') keepers. For Atwood, the writer has the massive responsibility of portraying, as vividly as possible, the bodily harm that silence and invisibility and neutrality can cause and tolerate. Whether through dreams, nightmares, hallucinations, visions, or experience, she demonstrates that writers, by observing closely, reflect and judge their worlds. Finally, she also shows us, movingly, convincingly, that communicating the visions of the imagination, telling stories, no matter how bleak they are, creates the possibility of better worlds. Beyond despair, the very act of writing demonstrates, unequivocally, our human will to survive, and our capacity to hope.

NOTES

[1] In chapter 2 of *Sub/Version*, I pointed out that in *Bodily Harm*, Atwood draws attention to Northrop Frye's frequently quoted question about Canadian literature: "Where is here?" (42).

[2] The Consul of *Under the Volcano* translates (incorrectly) from the Spanish a series of questions on a sign addressed to people visiting a Mexican garden: Why is it yours? . . . "You like this garden? . . . We evict those that destroy" (133).

[3] In Part Six, when Rennie asks Lora why the guards bother putting salt in their prisoners' tea, Lora responds: " 'Because they can' " (280).

[4] See the line "Before the taking of a toast and tea" ("The Love Song of J. Alfred Prufrock," in *The Waste Land* [10]), and the lines "Should I, after tea and cakes and ices, / Have the strength to force the moment to its crisis?" (12).

[5] In an unpublished interview, conducted at the Fisher Rare Book Library on 28 May 1985, Judith McCombs asked Atwood about some of her water-colours. Looking at the one that she had considered using for the cover of *Bodily Harm*, Atwood continued: "And what I finally did put on it in the Canadian version was a scientific drawing from the 19th century of a marine organism. A diat — [diatom] — one of those little things that float around in the ocean. And I wanted to make a — I wanted a cell, is what I wanted. And I looked at a number of photographs of cells, and none of them had what I wanted. So then I tried painting one myself and none of those had — although this might have been nice, with the lettering above and below" (30).

[6] Towards the end of "The Burial of the Dead" section of Eliot's *The Waste Land*, the poet describes an "Unreal City," where

Under the brown fog of a winter dawn,
A crowd flowed over London Bridge, so many,
I had not thought death had undone so many.

Sighs, short and infrequent, were exhaled,
And each man fixed his eyes before his feet.
(*The Waste Land* 29)

7 Again, *Bodily Harm* seems influenced by *The Waste Land* and the myths Eliot used. Dr. Minnow, a Christ figure, connects also with the Fisher King. Atwood said, in reference to a statement by Pierre Berton, that "I thought quite carefully about my male characters in *Bodily Harm*. . . . A female novelist and critic noted that there was one good man in the book and no good women, and she's quite right. . . . the *good* man is *black*, which is perhaps why the 'mean-to-menners' overlooked him" (sw 425). I suggest also that Atwood has used the Tarot cards, both visually and symbolically (see the lance and the cup, for example).

8 At the conclusion of the Mendez-Egle interview, Atwood said: "I've never had cancer. I wrote a whole book in which the character has had and probably still has" (Ingersoll 170).

Works Cited

Ager, Susan. Review. *San Jose Mercury* 29 Mar. 1982; Newsbank 1981–82, 91: D13–14.

Atherton, Stanley. "Tropical Traumas: Images of the Caribbean in Recent Canadian Fiction." *Canadian Literature* 95 (1982): 8–14. Describes *Bodily Harm*, in the context of other novels, as a depressing, alienated work, a nightmare.

Atwood, Margaret. *Dancing Girls (DG)*. Toronto: McClelland, 1977.

———. *Life Before Man (LBM)*. Toronto: McClelland, 1979.

———. *True Stories (TS)*. Toronto: Oxford UP, 1981.

———. *Bodily Harm (BH)*. Toronto: McClelland, 1981.

———. *Second Words: Selected Critical Prose (SW)*. Toronto: McClelland, 1982.

———. *Bluebeard's Egg (BE)*. Toronto: McClelland, 1983.

———. *Murder in the Dark: Short Fictions and Prose Poems (MD)*. Toronto: Coach House, 1983.

———. *The Handmaid's Tale (HT)*. Toronto: McClelland, 1985.

———. *The CanLit Foodbook (CLF)*. Toronto: Totem, 1987.

———. *Cat's Eye (CE)*. Toronto: McClelland, 1988.

———. "If You Can't Say Something Nice, Don't Say Anything At All." *Language in Her Eye: Writing and Gender*. Ed. Libby Scheier, Sarah Sheard & Eleanor Wachtel. Toronto: Coach House, 1990. 15–25.

Berger, Thomas. *Ways of Seeing*. Middlesex: Penguin, 1972.

Blaise, Clark. "Tale of Two Colonies." *Canadian Literature* 95 (1982): 110–12. In this review, Blaise compliments Atwood on catching the Toronto tone in *Bodily Harm* but argues that the Caribbean material is not well integrated.

Brydon, Diana. "Caribbean Revolution & Literary Convention." *Canadian Literature* 95 (1982): 181–85. As a parody of the imperialist novel, *Bodily Harm* shows how form and language control political opposition.

———. Review. *Westerly*. March 1982: 98–100.

Carrington, Ildikó de Papp. "Another Symbolic Descent." *Essays on Canadian Writing* 26 (1983): 45–63. An informed early discussion of major themes and images in *Bodily Harm*, showing the reality of suffering and evil.

————. "Margaret Atwood and Her Works." *Canadian Writers and Their Works*. Fiction Series. Vol. 9. Ed. Robert Lecker, Jack David, and Ellen Quigley. Toronto: ECW, 1987. 25–116. Emphasizes *Bodily Harm*'s satire and the writer's moral responsibility.

Castro, Jan. "An Interview with Margaret Atwood." *Margaret Atwood: Vision and Forms*. Ed. Kathryn VanSpanckeren and Jan Garden Castro. Carbondale: Southern Illinois UP, 1988. 215–32.

Davey, Frank. *Margaret Atwood: A Feminist Poetics*. The New Canadian Criticism Series. Vancouver: Talonbooks, 1984. Describes *Bodily Harm* as a traditional narrative, moving from alienation, through descent, to a positive return.

————. Review. *Canadian Forum* 61 (1981): 29–30.

Davidson, Arnold. "The Poetics of Pain in Margaret Atwood's *Bodily Harm*." *The American Review of Canadian Studies* 18 (1988): 1–10. A pointed analysis of Atwood's avoidance of escapist endings as this concern reveals more intense political commitment.

Eliot, T.S. *The Waste Land and Other Poems*. London: Faber, 1940.

Finn, Geraldine. "Feminism and Fiction: In Praise of Praxis, Beyond Bodily Harm." *Socialist Studies: A Canadian Annual* (1983): 51–78. In *Bodily Harm*, Atwood fails to be revolutionary because of maintaining the illusion of realism.

Forceville, C., A. Fry, and P. de Voogd, eds. *External and Detached: Dutch Essays on Contemporary Canadian Literature*. Amsterdam: Free UP, 1988.

Forché, Carolyn. *The Country Between Us*. New York: Harper, 1981.

Gillen, Francis (Moderator). "A Conversation: Margaret Atwood and Students." *Margaret Atwood: Vision and Form*. Ed. Kathryn VanSpanckeren and Jan Garden Castro. Carbondale: Southern Illinois UP, 1988. 233–43.

Goodwin, Ken. "Revolution as Bodily Harm: Thea Astley and Margaret Atwood." *Antipodes: A North American Journal of Australian Literature*. (1990): 109–15. Emphasizes the two-way metaphor of state and body; includes copies of two Atwood water-colors, with a following note by Sharon Wilson.

Guckengerger, Katherine. Review. *Cincinnati Enquirer* 11 Apr. 1982; Newsbank 1981–82, 80: C7.

Hales, Leslie-Ann. "Genesis Revisited: The Darkening Vision of Margaret Atwood." *The Month*. July 1987: 257–62. Sees *Bodily Harm* as a transitional text, categorically rejecting men.

Halligan, Marion. Review. *Canberra Times* 18 Sept. 1982: 14.

Hancock, Geoff. *Canadian Writers at Work: Interviews*. Toronto: Oxford UP, 1987.

Hansen, Elaine Tuttle. "Fiction and (Post) Feminism in Atwood's *Bodily Harm*." *Novel: A Forum on Fiction* 19.1 (1985): 5–21. An astute, close reading of the novel that raises questions about consciousness-raising and writing as instigators of social change.

Harpur, Tom. "Atwood's Priority: How Do We Stop War?" *The Toronto Star* 5 Oct. 1981: D1, D3.

Hosek, Chaviva. "Margaret Atwood's *Bodily Harm*." *World Literature Written in English* 22 (1983): 287–90. Complains about Atwood's appropriation of Alice Munro country, and the narrator's flat voice.

Howe, Linda. "Narratives of Survival." *The Literary Review* 26.1 (1982): 177–84. The author takes Rennie on a metaphorical journey through Hell, which Rennie survives.

Howells, Coral Ann. "Worlds Alongside: Contradictory Discourses in the Fiction of Alice Munro and Margaret Atwood." *Gaining Ground: European Critics on Canadian Literature*. Ed. Robert Kroetsch and Reginald Nischik. Edmonton: NeWest, 1985. 121–36. Reads *Bodily Harm* as traditional gothic, transforming fantasy into realism.

———. *Private and Fictional Worlds: Canadian Women Novelists of the 1970s and 1980s*. London: Methuen, 1987. 53–70. Argues that Atwood is at her most radical in *Bodily Harm*, in generic, gender and national terms.

Hutcheon, Linda. *The Canadian Postmodern: A Study of Contemporary English-Canadian Fiction*. Studies in Canadian Literature. Toronto: Oxford UP, 1988. Perceptive comments about process and product as these apply to the politically committed *Bodily Harm*.

Ingersoll, Earl. *Margaret Atwood: Conversations*. Princeton: Ontario Review, 1990. A collection of major interviews. The most relevant to *Bodily Harm* are those with Margaret Kaminski (1975); Linda Sandler (1976); Jim Davidson (1978); Karla Hammond (1978 and 1979); Jo Brans (1982); Beatrice Mendez-Egle (1983); Elizabeth Meese (1985); and Bonnie Lyons (1987).

Irvine, Lorna. *Sub/Version*. Toronto: ECW, 1986. 37–53. Discussion of various levels of meaning in *Bodily Harm*. Rpt.in a slightly different version as "The Here and Now of *Bodily Harm*." *Margaret Atwood: Vision and Forms*. Ed. Kathryn VanSpanckeren and Jan Garden Castro. Carbondale: Southern Illinois UP, 1988. 85–100).

Jaidev. Review. *Newstime* 21 Oct. 1984: n. pag.

Jones, Dorothy. " 'Waiting for the Rescue': A discussion of Margaret Atwood's *Bodily Harm*." *Kunapipi* 6.3 (1984): 86–100. A thorough, interesting analysis of religious imagery in the novel.

Kareda, Urjo. Review. *Saturday Night* 96 (1981): 70, 72.

Keith, W.J. *A Sense of Style: Studies in the Art of Fiction in English-Speaking Canada*. Toronto: ECW, 1989. Sees *Bodily Harm* as an ambitious, frequently didactic novel, that suffers artistically.

Ketcham, Diane. Review. *Oakland Tribune* 28 Mar. 1982; Newsbank 1981–82, 80: C2–3.

Kirchhoff, H.J. Interview with Atwood. *[Toronto] Globe and Mail* 15 Oct. 1988. C13.

Kirtz, Mary. "The Thematic Imperative: Didactic Characterization in *Bodily Harm*." *Margaret Atwood: Reflection and Reality*. Ed. Beatrice Mendez-Egle. Edinburg, TX: Pan American UP, 1987. 116–30. Argues that multi-layered references to hands signify the novel's major image pattern.

Kroetsch, Robert and Reginald Nischik, eds. *Gaining Ground: European Critics on Canadian Literature*. Western Canadian Literary Documents Ser. 6. Edmonton: NeWest, 1985.

Langer, Beryl. "Class and Gender in Margaret Atwood's Fiction." *Australian-Canadian Studies* 6.1 (1988): 73–101. Emphasizes the social, moral and economic tensions experienced by Atwood's new transition class in *Bodily Harm*.

Leonard, John. Review *New York Times Book Review* 21 Mar. 1982: 3,20–21.

Lipscomb, Elizabeth Johnston. Rev. of *Bodily Harm*. *Magill's Literary Annual* 1 (1983): 65–69. Comments on the novel's stereotypes and layered complexities.

Lowry, Malcolm. *Under The Volcano*. 1947. London: Penguin, 1962.

MacDonald, Larry. "Psychologism and the Philosophy of Progress: The Recent Fiction of MacLennan, Davies and Atwood." *Studies in Canadian Literature* (1984): 121–43. Accuses Atwood of reducing social evil to mental illness and thus conflating subjectivity and objectivity.

McCombs Judith, ed. *Critical Essays on Margaret Atwood*. Critical Essays on World Literature. Boston: G.K. Hall, 1988.

——— . "Country, Politics and Gender in Canadian Studies: A Report From Twenty Years of Atwood Criticism." *Canadian Issues / Themes canadiens* 10.5 (1988): 27–47. Mentions a number of reviews and critiques of *Bodily Harm* up to 1987.

McCombs, Judith, and Carole L. Palmer. *Margaret Atwood: A Reference Guide*. Boston: G.K. Hall, 1992.

McDougall, Robert, and Gillian Whitlock, eds. *Australian/Canadian Literatures in English: Comparative Perspectives*. Australia: Methuen, 1987.

Mellors, John. Review. *London Magazine* June 1982: 61–65.

Mendez-Egle, Beatrice, and James M. Haule, eds. *Margaret Atwood: Reflection and Reality*. Living Authors Series 6. Edinburg, TX: Pan American UP, 1987.

Moore, M. L. Review. *Epoch* 32 (1983): 169–73. Suggests that Rennie is a "secularized Dante" who unfortunately does not change.

Patton, Marilyn. "Tourists and Terrorists: The Creation of *Bodily Harm*."

Papers on Language and Literature. Edwardsville: Southern Illinois, UP, 1991. Helpful analysis of the increasingly political dimensions of Atwood's writing; uses archival material.

Powe, B.W. *A Climate Charged: Essays on Canadian Writers.* Oakville ON: Mosaic, 1984. An acerbic atttack on Atwood's trendinesss; in *Bodily Harm,* process eclipses product, producing stalemated characters.

Rainwater, Catherine. "The Sense of the Flesh in Four Novels by Margaret Atwood." *Margaret Atwood: Reflection and Reality.* Ed. Beatrice Mendez-Egle. Edinburg, TX: Pan American UP, 1987. 14–28. Through a four-stage process, *Bodily Harm* demonstrates an alteration in its main character's physical boundaries.

Rankin, Jennifer. *Earth Hold.* London: Secker and Warburg, 1978.

Rigney, Barbara Hill. *Margaret Atwood.* Women Writers. London: MacMillan Education, 1987. Argues that *Bodily Harm* stresses the importance of vision and of female bonding.

Robinson, Jill. Review. *Chicago Tribune* 28 Mar. 1982; Newsbank 1981–82, 80: C5.

Rosenberg, Jerome. *Margaret Atwood.* Twayne's World Authors Ser. Boston: Twayne, 1984. Sees *Bodily Harm* as a work of "political realism" that is profoundly pessimistic.

Rubenstein, Roberta. "Pandora's Box and Female Survival: Margaret Atwood's *Bodily Harm.*" *Journal of Canadian Studies* 20.1 (1985): 120–35. Rpt. in *Critical Essays on Margaret Atwood.* Ed. Judith McCombs. Boston: G.K. Hall, 1988. 259–75. Points out parallels between events and symbols, emphasizing that cancer functions as a "scourge of the body" and a metaphor for diseases of "the body politic."

———. *Boundaries of the Self: Gender, Culture, Fiction.* Chicago: U. of Illinois P, 1987. Demonstrates Rennie's divided body and the novel's three distinct narrative strands.

Scheier, Libby, Sarah Sheard, and Eleanor Wachtel, eds. *Language in Her Eye: Writing and Gender.* Toronto: Coach House, 1990.

See, Carolyn. Review. *Los Angeles Times* 22 Mar. 1982: sec.5: 6.

Smith, Rowland. "Margaret Atwood and the City: Style and Substance in *Bodily Harm* and *Bluebeard's Egg.*" *World Literature Written in English* 25 (1985): 252–64. Stresses the novel's macabre humor and its sardonic texture.

Stovel, Nora Foster. "Reflections on Mirror Images: Doubles and Identity in the Novels of Margaret Atwood." *Essays on Canadian Writing* 33 (1986): 50–67. Mirrors in *Bodily Harm* are metaphorical, rather than literal; novel moves through solipsism to community.

Strauss, Jennifer. " 'Everyone is in Politics': Margaret Atwood's *Bodily Harm* and Blanche d'Alpuget's *Turtle Beach.*" *Australian/Canadian Literatures in*

English. Ed. Robert McDougall and Gillian Whitlock. Australia: Methuen, 1987. 111–19. Sees *Bodily Harm* as essentially realistic, with a closed ending; asks whether "here" is a country of the mind.

Tiffin, Helen. "Voice and Form." *Australian/Canadian Literatures in English*. Ed. Robert McDougall and Gillian Whitlock. Australia: Methuen, 1987. 119–32. Disagrees with Strauss's reading of *Bodily Harm*, arguing that problems exist with the monocultural perspective and the distance between narrator and author.

Twigg, Alan. *For Openers: Conversations with 24 Writers*. Madeira Park, BC: Harbour, 1981. 219–30. Rpt. in *Margaret Atwood: Conversations*. Ed. Earl Ingersoll. Princeton: Ontario Review, 1990. 121–30.

Tyler, Ann. Review. *Detroit News* 4 Apr. 1982: M2.

VanSpanckeren, Kathryn, and Jan Garden Castro, eds. *Margaret Atwood: Vision and Forms*. Ad Feminam Ser. Carbondale: Southern Illinois UP, 1988.

Voogd, Peter J. de. "A Handmaid's Harm: Or, Margaret Atwood's Dystopia." *External and Detached: Dutch Essays on Contemporary Canadian Literature*. Ed. C. Forceville, A. Fry, P. de Voogd. Amsterdam: Free UP, 1988. 29–35. Argues that *Bodily Harm* is a better novel than *The Handmaid's Tale*.

Wainwright, J.A. Review. *Dalhousie Review* 61 (1981): 581–83. Complains about Rennie's naïveté and Atwood's didacticism.

Wilson, Sharon. "Turning Life into Popular Art: *Bodily Harm*'s Life-Tourist." *Studies in Canadian Literature* 10.1 & 2 (1985): 136–45. Emphasizes the various levels of "tourist vision" in the novel.

———. "Camera Images in Margaret Atwood's Novels." *Margaret Atwood: Reflection and Reality*. Ed. Beatrice Mendez-Egle. Edinburg, TX: Pan American UP, 1987. 29–57. Points out four main functions of camera images, showing how these comment on *Bodily Harm*'s meaning.

———. "A Note on Margaret Atwood's Visual Art and *Bodily Harm*." *Antipodes: A North American Journal of Australian Literature* (1990): 115–16. Discusses how two of Atwood's water-colors ("Untitled Watercolor of a Microscope Image," and "Amanita Caesarea, Egg, Cross-Section on Cloud") relate to *Bodily Harm*.

I have used *The Newsletter of the Margaret Atwood Society* (1984–90), particularly Carole L. Palmer's valuable Checklist of Atwood Scholarship (1986–90). The *Newsletter* is published annually: Ed. Jerome Rosenberg, Dept. of English, Miami University, Oxford, Ohio. I have also consulted the Atwood Archives, Thomas Fisher Rare Book Library, Toronto: Boxes 7–8; 33–39; 58; 63–65; 69; 74; 76; 78; 95.

Index